Animal Rights and Wrongs

Animal Rights and Wrongs

Third Edition published in association with DEM⊙S

Roger Scruton

metro

First published in 1996 (second edition in 1998)
by Demos, 9 Bridewell Place, London EC4V 6AP

This third edition published in Great Britain in 2000
by Metro Books (an imprint of Metro Publishing Limited),
19 Gerrard Street, London W1V 7LA,
in association with Demos

Text © 1996, 1998, 2000 Demos

British Library Cataloguing in Publication Data.
A CIP record of this book is available on request
from the British Library.

ISBN 1 900512 81 5

10 9 8 7 6 5 4 3 2 1

Typeset by Textype Typesetters, Cambridge
Printed in Great Britain by Caledonian International Book
Manufacturing, Glasgow

CONTENTS

Preface   *vii*

1 ● Metaphysics   *1*

2 ● The Moral Being   *27*

3 ● Life, Death, Joy and Suffering   *39*

4 ● The Moral Margin   *51*

5 ● The Roots of Moral Thinking   *57*

6 ● The Rational Basis of Moral Judgement   *69*

7 ● The Moral Status of Animals   *79*

8 ● Duty and the Beast: Moral Conclusions   *123*

9 ● Morality and the Law   *135*

Appendix 1: Thoughts on Farming   *139*

Appendix 2: Thoughts on Hunting   *147*

Appendix 3: Thoughts on Fishing   *165*

Glossary of Philosophical Terms   *173*

Notes   *191*

Index   *199*

PREFACE

The first edition of this book was published by the independent think-tank Demos in 1996. This new edition has been revised and expanded to take account of recent events, in particular the debate over hunting with hounds and the crisis in livestock farming. Hunting has been heatedly condemned, largely by people who know nothing about it: for this reason I have added an appendix on the subject, in order to raise the debate to the level where some glimmer of understanding might dawn. However, hunting is not my primary concern. This book is philosophical, an attempt to discover the principles which could answer the many moral dilemmas presented by our relations with other species, rather than an attempt to answer them one by one.

Moreover, from the moral point of view, the situation of livestock is of far greater concern than that of the fox. The BSE crisis led to the mass slaughter of healthy animals and dealt a severe blow to the feelings that attach farmers to their animals, so threatening the principal source of a cattle-herd's protection. The subsequent collapse of livestock farming in Britain has led to calves, lambs and ewes being abandoned by farmers who can afford neither to keep them nor to have them killed. Regulations governing slaughter, interpreted by MAFF in a manner that reflects an institutionalised hostility to the small producer, have forced the closure of local abattoirs, so further undermining the conditions which make it possible for a farmer to take full responsibility for the animals in his care. In response to these and related developments, I have included another appendix on farming, in which I question some of the moral assumptions implicit in current policy and in the public attitude to the production of meat.

It is not only hunting and meat production that have awakened the defenders of 'animal rights'. Cat lovers have recently so persecuted the owner of a cat farm as to force the closure of his enterprise; cats necessary for medical experiments must now be imported from places where they are raised far less kindly. Campaigners have released mink from fur farms into the wild, causing immense damage to local wildlife and exposing the mink themselves to shooting, trapping or starvation. Fur farming has itself come under attack in Parliament, even though nobody has been able to explain why raising animals for their fur is more heinous than raising them for their meat.

Organisations like the RSPCA, the International Fund for Animal Welfare and PETA (People for the Ethical Treatment of Animals) devote prodigious resources to the attempt to abolish fox-hunting, seal-hunting, deer-hunting, angling and shooting, while ignoring altogether the argument that these activities, properly conducted, do more to conserve habitats and species than any amount of sentimental concern for the individual victim. Such blindness to the fate of species may have been excusable in a world where man was a subordinate part of the natural order. But man is now in control. The result is a progressive destruction of the habitats of almost all wild animals apart from suburban scavengers. Those who campaign against traditional and environmentally friendly forms of stewardship, while being completely indifferent to the question what might be put in their place, can scarcely claim the moral high ground in the debate over the treatment of wild animals.

Public discussion meanwhile has become ever more confused. In my view the confusion has a metaphysical cause. People lack the concepts that would enable them to understand the deep differences between animals and humans. The old ideas of the soul, free-will and eternal judgement, which made the distinction between people and animals so important and so clear, have lost their authority, and nothing adequate has come in place of them. Creatures were once divided into those with a rational soul and those without one. Now the division is between pets and pests, distinguished not by their habits, but by their appearance. Pets are granted honorary status of the human community, itself Disneyfied to include them. Among pets, therefore, are counted the deer, the fox, the badger and the mink — four of the most destructive animals at large in our countryside. Among pests we find the toad, the water rat, the grass-snake and the spider — all four of them useful to mankind, vital to the ecological system, and in steady decline. In the eyes of many otherwise rational and decent people, rats may be used in medical experiments, but not cats; mice may be hunted by cats, but not foxes by hounds; chickens may be kept in cramped cages, but not calves; pigs may be raised for their meat, but not dogs.

It goes without saying that this division between the pet and the pest has no basis in reality. Nor is it of any help to the animals themselves, who can benefit from our treatment only if they are not forced to behave as honorary members of the human species. At no time in human history have animals stood in greater need of our protection; and at no time has the protection been offered and withdrawn on such arbitrary and self-indulgent grounds. Clearly, therefore, there is a need for a scrupulous and moral approach to other species. This book is an attempt to say what that involves.

I have tried to make the argument intelligible to readers with little or no knowledge of philosophy. In order to do so, however, I have had to remove from the text all finicky questions of definition and scholarship. Hence, in addition to the appendices on farming, hunting and fishing, I have provided a glossary of philosophical terms, in which the reader will find definitions and explanations of all the technical idioms occurring in the body of the text.

I have greatly benefited from discussions with Jim Barrington, Bob Grant, Sophie Scruton, Geoff Mulgan, Geoffrey Thomas and David Wiggins. Like many of those who have ventured into this area, I am indebted to creatures who have no idea of the fact – to Puck, who used to guard the gate, to George, Sam and Rollo, who lived in the stables, to the nameless carp in the pond across the field, to the cows next door and to Herbie, who has now been eaten.

Malmesbury, October 1999

METAPHYSICS

Animals were once regarded as things, placed on earth for our use and enjoyment, to be treated according to our convenience. This is no longer so. All thinking people now recognise the gulf that exists between sentient and non-sentient beings and almost all recognise that we have no God-given right to ignore the suffering that we cause just because the victim belongs to some other species. Some, however, go further than this, extending to animals the rights that have until now been reserved for humans. In 1965, Brigid Brophy published 'The rights of animals' in the *Sunday Times*, consciously harking back to Tom Paine and the *Rights of Man*; in 1975, with the publication of *Animal Liberation*, the Australian philosopher Peter Singer outlined the case, as he saw it, for a complete rethinking of our relations to other species. Meanwhile, Richard Ryder had introduced the term 'speciesism' in order to imply that, like racism and sexism, our attitude to other animals is a form of unjust discrimination, lacking both rational basis and moral title. These writers have so changed the climate of opinion that no thinking person could now treat animals as our ancestors did, ignoring their feelings and desires and thinking only of their human uses. In a world dominated by humans and their appetites, animals are now widely perceived as a victim class.

Nevertheless, it seems to me that the philosophical case mounted by Peter Singer, Tom Regan, Richard Ryder and others has no real cogency. I do not wish to denigrate their achievement in awakening the world to needless cruelties and in compelling us to rethink so many comfortable prejudices. On the other hand, their single-minded emphasis on the features which humans share with other animals – notably, on the capacity for suffering – causes them to overlook the distinction between moral beings (to whom their argument is addressed) and the rest of nature. Since traditional morality is based on this distinction, it cannot be revised by arguments which so blithely ignore it. It seems to me, indeed, that the *philosophical* discussion of our duties to animals has recently been conducted at a level which gives no real grounds for any conclusion – certainly no grounds for the quite radical conclusions drawn by Singer, Regan and Ryder.

This is not to say that all is right with our traditional morality. But if we are to know what is right with it and what is wrong, we must explore the roots of moral thinking and try to discover exactly how it is, in such a case, that questions of right and wrong could be decided. In what follows I present a map of the territory. Every issue that I touch on is hotly debated and to explore all the philosophical arguments would be not only tedious to the reader but also destructive of my purpose, which is to help those who are genuinely puzzled by the question of animal welfare to see how it *might* be answered by someone who takes it as seriously as a philosopher ought. At the very least, I hope to show that you can love animals and still believe that, in the right circumstances, it is morally permissible to eat them, to hunt them, to keep them as pets, to wear their skins and even to use them in experiments. The real question is not *whether* we should do those things but *when* and *how*.

THE PROBLEM

If we ask ourselves why the question of animals and their welfare should have risen so prominently to consciousness in recent times, we must surely identify the decline in religious belief as a vital factor. So long as people were sure of their status as the highest order of creation, made in God's image, blessed with an immortal soul and destined for judgement and eternity, they had no difficulty in rationalising the difference between themselves and other animals or in justifying standards of treatment for the latter which, if applied to the former, would have been criminal or worse.[1] It is no part of my purpose to argue against the theological view of human life. But the least that can be said is that it is both controversial in itself and of dwindling influence over the thoughts and feelings of modern people. Although the idea of a purely secular morality remains problematic, we cannot hope for guidance in the circumstances of modern life if we do not explore the grounds of moral judgement in terms acceptable to unbelievers. It may be true that the very great moral difficulties that surround us – including this one, concerning our duties to other animals – have come about precisely because of the secularisation of modern society and of the 'Enlightenment project', as Alasdair MacIntyre has described it,[2] of deriving morality from reason alone. But this would make it all the more urgent to address moral questions in terms which make no theological assumptions.

The problems that I shall be discussing arise because we are animals, but animals of a very special kind – animals who are conscious of themselves as individuals, with rights, responsibilities and duties, and who are capable of extending their sympathy to other species. From a biological point of view, the species are grouped under kinds, with radically different evolutionary histories and radically different ways of relating to the environment. These biological distinctions greatly influence our responses to the animal kingdom. Towards insects we have little sympathy; reptiles and fish delight us but inspire no affection; mammals in general (or at least the larger mammals) prompt our warm concern. Beneath all those varieties lie forms of animal life, from slug to tapeworm, which appear to us merely as parts of the machinery of nature, to be dealt with according to *our* interests and with no special regard for *theirs*. To suppose that there is a single answer to the question, 'How should we treat the animals?', when both biological science and ordinary sentiment recognise such vast divisions among them, would be to take the kind of mechanical approach to the problem against which people are now in rebellion. At the same time, it is hard to decide whether there is any rational basis for the *moral* distinctions that we seem to make among species or whether we are guided by anything more than anthropomorphic sentiment in looking so coldly on those creatures, like fish and insects, which look coldly on us.

An element of favouritism is bound to enter into our dealings with the animal kingdom and it would be wrong to suppose that this is unjust. Those species which contribute most to our domestic happiness – such as dog, cat and horse, with whom it is almost as if we have long-standing treaties of mutual aid – are bound to secure preferential treatment and it would show a lack of conscience to withhold it. Those which elicit instinctive reactions of disgust will inevitably lose out in the race for human protection. Few people who object to hunting foxes with hounds oppose catching rats with terriers. Despite their intelligence, warm attachments and interest in the surrounding world, rats – who, in modern conditions, are no more of a nuisance than foxes – do not have the right appearance. Try as we might, our instinctive disgust at the sight of their scaly tails, their low-slung bodies and their rapid scuffling movements, neutralise our sympathy. It is only their remarkable proficiency in breeding that has enabled them to hold their own against the accumulated weight of human revulsion.

This is not to condone such discriminations but merely to take note of them as a factor in the moral equation. The higher forms of animal life depend on us for their survival. It is because we breed them, feed them, preserve their habitats or domesticate them for our uses that they are able to win out in the stiff competition for resources, in a world now dominated by humans. Those which fail to elicit our strongest sympathy must either breed like the rat or sink rapidly towards extinction, like the snakes, lizards and toads that once abounded in our countryside and which are now only rarely encountered. No doubt a fully reasoned response to the moral question will take issue with many of our instinctive sympathies and it is not to be supposed that reasonable people, having taken note of all the relevant considerations, will find their prejudices unchanged. Nevertheless, there are unavoidable constraints imposed by human nature and anyone who defended a moral scheme in which rats, lizards and cockroaches took precedence over cats and dogs would be rightly ignored. Perhaps this means that a fully systematic code of conduct towards the animals will never be achieved. However, it is still possible both to respect our instinctive sympathies and to introduce into them such revisions as may be necessary to ensure that those species which do not attract us will nevertheless find a niche in our world.

In what follows, I shall consider the kinds of animal which attract our normal interest and sympathy. I shall assume that most, if not all, of the stranger forms of animal life – worms, fleas, locusts and so on – are not in the same way suitors for our moral concern. They interest us primarily as species and only rarely as individuals.

THE MINDS OF ANIMALS

Suppose that we set aside all theological speculation and accept in broad outline the Darwinian theory of species. The animal kingdom then appears as a many-branched tree, with ourselves at the furthest point along one of the branches. Our nearest neighbours, the higher primates, are so like us in appearance and so able and willing to ape our interests that we find it difficult at times not to look on them as we look on human children. Further down the branch we find animals which are remote from us in appearance and, by comparison, intellectually and emotionally impoverished. On other branches we find animals like the ant and the bee, whose collective life surpasses in order and discipline anything that we could achieve, yet to which we might hesitate to apply words like 'belief', 'desire' and 'intellect' and which display only a metallic caricature of our human feelings. On yet other branches we find animals which have no social life at all or whose social feelings extend no further than is required by the needs of reproduction.

The most pressing question posed by this picture is that of the mental life of our nearest neighbours. To what extent do these animals have minds? Descartes, for whom the mind was coextensive with self-consciousness, found himself compelled to argue that animals are living machines, in which bodily events are accompanied by no mental processes.[3] Neither philosophers nor zoologists would now accept that view; indeed, they would see it merely as one of the many unacceptable consequences of the Cartesian theory of the mind – the theory caricatured by Ryle as that of the 'ghost in the machine'.[4] The common-sense view, that the higher animals have a mental life which is importantly similar to ours, is now also a commonplace among philosophers. And not only among modern philosophers. Aristotle used one word – *psuche* – to denote the animating principle in all forms of life (including the life of plants). Reason and self-consciousness belong to *nous*, which is the immortal part of *psuche*.

The favoured modern approach is far nearer to Aristotle than to Descartes. Like Aristotle, modern philosophers would argue that human beings are distinguished only by the *level* of their mental life and not by the fact of it. For the mind is the cause of activity and is as much a part of the natural world as the activity which it explains. We understand the mind not by looking inwards but by studying cognitive and sensory behaviour. And we cannot study this behaviour without noticing the enormous structural similarities between human and animal life.

We can arrange mental life in a hierarchy of levels; an animal may exhibit activity of a lower level without displaying the marks of a higher, but not vice versa. Intuitively, the levels might be identified as follows.

- *The sensory:* animals have sensations — they feel things, react to things, exhibit pain, irritation and the sensations of hot and cold. Maybe animals such as molluscs exist only at this level. Still, this fact is enough for us to take account of their experience, even if we do not weep like the walrus as we scrape the raw oyster from its shell and sting its wounds with lemon juice.
- *The perceptual:* animals also perceive things — by sight, hearing, smell and touch. Perception is a higher state than sensation; it involves not just a response to the outer world but an assessment of it. Our disposition to think of animals as perceiving things is greatly influenced by the fact that they share with us many of the organs of perception, including the eye, the nose and the ear. They also

exhibit attention, in which eye, nose or ear are 'strained' towards the world in search of information.

- *The appetitive:* animals have appetites and needs and go in search of the things that fulfil them – whether it be food, water or sexual stimulus. They also have aversions: they flee from cold, discomfort and the threat of predators. Appetite and aversion can be observed in all organisms which also have perceptual powers – in slugs and worms, as well as birds, bees and bulldogs. But only in some of these cases can we speak also of desire. Desire belongs to a higher order of mental activity: it requires not just a response to the perceived situation, but a definite belief about it.
- *The cognitive:* some animals have beliefs. There are philosophers who doubt this point. Nevertheless, it is impossible to relate in any effective way to the higher animals unless we take account of what they think is going on in their environment. The dog thinks it is about to be taken for a walk; the cat thinks there is a mouse behind the wall; the stag thinks there is a ditch beyond the hedge and makes due allowance as it jumps. In using such language, I am attributing beliefs to the animals in question. To put it in another way: I am not just describing the animal's behaviour; I am also making room for an evaluation of it, as true or false. The dog, cat or stag might well be mistaken. And to say that such an animal has beliefs is to imply not just that it can

make mistakes, but that it can also learn from them.

Learning involves acquiring and losing beliefs on the basis of a changed assessment of the situation; it involves *recognising* objects, places and other animals; it involves *expecting* familiar things and being surprised by novelties. An animal which learns adapts its behaviour to changes in the environment: hence, with the concept of belief come those of recognition, expectation and surprise.

Learning is therefore not to be thought of in terms of the 'conditioning' made familiar by behaviourist psychology. The process of conditioning – the association of a repeated stimulus with a 'learned' response – can be observed in forms of life that have not yet risen to the cognitive level. Conditioning involves a change in behaviour but not necessarily a change of mind. It has been abundantly shown that the higher animals acquire new behaviour not merely by conditioning but in innovative ways: taking short cuts to the right conclusion, making intuitive connections, swimming to a place which they had known only through walking or recognising with their eyes the prey that they had been following by nose.

When describing behaviour of this kind – cognitive behaviour – we make unavoidable reference to the content of a mental state: the proposition whose truth is in question. The terrier believes that the rat is in the hole, it is surprised that the hole is empty; it sees that the rat is running across the floor of the barn and so on. In all such cases the word 'that' – one of the most difficult, from the point of view of logic, in the language – introduces the content of the terrier's state of mind. The use of this term is forced on us by the phenomenon; but once we have begun to use it, we have crossed a barrier in the order of things. We have begun to attribute mental states which are 'about' the world and which are focused upon a proposition. The term 'intentionality' (from Latin *intendere*, to aim) has been adopted to describe the 'aboutness' of our mental states – not because there is any agreement concerning its explanation but because it calls out for a name. Without going further into the matter, it seems to me clear that intentionality introduces not merely a new level of mental life but also the first genuine claim of the animals upon our sympathies and our moral concern. For it distinguishes those animals which merely react to a stimulus from those which react to the *idea* of a stimulus. Animals of the second kind have minds which importantly resemble ours: there is a view of the world which is theirs, an assessment of reality which we ourselves can alter. It is therefore possible to relate to a creature with inten-tionality, as we do not and cannot relate to a creature without it. An animal with intentionality is one to which we can appeal and which therefore can appeal to us.

This partly explains the great difference between

our response to insects and our response to the higher mammals. Although insects perceive things, their perception funds no changing store of beliefs but simply forms part of the link between stimulus and response. If the stimulus is repeated, so too is the response, regardless of the consequences – as when a moth flies into the candle flame, not out of stupidity or heroism, but because this is what happens when it perceives the light. Moths learn nothing from this experience and have no store of information as a result of their past perceptions. They end life as they began it, in a state of cognitive innocence from which no experience can tempt them.

By contrast, dogs, cats and the higher mammals have an understanding of reality which motivates their behaviour. They learn from their perceptions and we can share parts of our world view with them. We can even join with them in a common enterprise, as when a shepherd and his dog work side by side.

Desires and emotions

All animals have appetites and drives; but only some animals have desires. Desire, like belief, belongs to the cognitive level of mental life. Desires are intentional states – aiming at a goal and inspired by thought. The horse which desires to regain its stable is not the blind victim of a compulsion – unlike the mussels which 'slope their slow passage to the fallen flood'. For one thing, the desire of the horse can conflict with other desires and lose in the contest – as when the horse sees its stable-mate trotting in the opposite direction and gives up its schemes to make for home. Moreover, the horse's desire is goal-directed. It will choose different routes and strategies depending on its assessment of where it is, of how determined is its rider to resist it and of what obstacles bar its way.

Desire depends upon belief and belief is expressed in desire. From the combination of the two springs emotion, by which I mean a motive which is also a feeling. Fear motivates me to flee; it is also something that I feel in the face of danger. While insects are averse to predators, their aversion is of the stimulus-response variety and involves no assessment of the danger. An antelope which sniffs a leopard is suddenly 'alert to the danger'; its store of information is revised and with it the antelope's desires. No longer concerned only to eat the shrubs in front of it, the antelope tenses its limbs for flight and has one all-consuming desire – to be where this danger is not. This is a paradigm case of animal emotion and it shows the way in which emotions like fear are composed from beliefs, desires and the general readiness of the organism to protect its vital interests.

Animal emotions are drawn, however, from a narrow repertoire. The emotions that a creature can feel are limited by the thoughts that it can think. A bull may feel rage but not indignation or contempt. A lion may feel sexual urges but not erotic love. This fact is all-important in deciding on the moral status of animals; for our relations with others depend largely on our assessment of their emotional character. Of course, we have a tendency to read animal behaviour in terms of our own emotions; but this anthropomorphic habit must be set aside if we are to understand the real nature of animal motivation. The wasp is not angry at the violation of its nest and its sting is not an act of revenge or punishment. Nor is it anger that motivates the guard-dog or the rutting stag. For anger is founded on the thought that one has been wronged, and this is a thought which lies outside the intellectual repertoire of animals such as dogs and stags.

Animals may nevertheless be prompted by social feelings. A horse will want to run when the herd is running. It may try to be first in the field and display the kind of cockiness, as it muscles its way to the front, that is familiar to us from human teams, gangs and football crowds. Dogs respond in a social way to one another and also to humans. A dog is attentive to its master and seeks affection and approval, often engaging in quite unnatural exploits in the belief that these are required of it. It is almost impossible to observe the social feelings of animals without feeling a deep sense of kinship; when we too are included in the pack, flock or herd, we naturally reciprocate with gestures of fellowship. However anthropomorphic and ill-founded, these gestures make room in our world for the more sociable animals and bestow on them a kind of honorary membership of the human community.

RATIONALITY

Classical philosophers, notably Plato and Aristotle, describe human beings as rational animals, identifying reason as our distinguishing mark and implying that our mental life exists at an altogether higher level than that of the other animals.[5] Later philosophers, including Aquinas, Kant and Hegel, endorse the suggestion and it is one that is intrinsically appealing. However, it is not easy to say what it means. Definitions of reason and rationality vary greatly; so greatly as to suggest that, while pretending to define the difference between humans and animals in terms of reason, philosophers are really defining reason in terms of the difference between humans and animals. On one understanding at least, many of the higher animals *are* rational. They solve problems, choose appropriate means to their ends and adjust their beliefs according to the evidence of their senses.

Nevertheless, there are capacities which we have and the lower animals do not and which endow our mental life with much of its importance. Unlike the lower animals, we have a need and an ability to *justify* our beliefs and actions and to enter into reasoned dialogue with others. This need and ability seem to underlie all the many different ways in which we diverge from the lower animals. If we survey our mental life and examine the many specific differences between us and our nearest relations, we seem always to be exploring different facets of a single ontological divide – that between reasoning and non-reasoning beings. Here are some of the distinctions:

- Dogs, apes and bears have desires but they do not make choices. When we train an animal, we do so by inducing new desires, not by getting it to see that it should change its ways. We, by contrast, can choose to do what we do not want and want to do what we do not choose. Because of this, we can discuss together what is right or best to do, ignoring our desires.

    The 'punishments' administered during the training of an animal are therefore not really punishments. We are not seeking confession, contrition or remorse but simply a change of behaviour, regardless of right and wrong. Punishment of a person, by contrast, implies moral judgement. It forms part of the complex practice whereby guilt is assigned and acknowledged and trespassers are first expelled from the moral community and then readmitted, purged of their fault.

- The beliefs and desires of animals concern present objects: perceived dangers, immediate needs and so on. They do not make judgements about the past and future, or engage in long-term planning. Squirrels store food for the winter but they are guided by instinct rather than a rational plan. (To put it another way: if this is a project, it is one that the squirrel *cannot change*, no more than an ant could resign from its community and set up shop on its own.) Animals *remember* things and in that way retain beliefs about the past: but about the past as it affects the present. As Schopenhauer argues,[6] the recollection of animals is confined to what they perceive: it involves the recognition of familiar things. They remember only what is prompted by the present experience; they do not 'read the past' but 'live in a world of perception'.

- Animals relate to one another but not as we do. They growl and feint, until their territories are certain; but they recognise no right of property, no sovereignty, no duty to give way. They do not criticise one another, nor do they engage in the give and take of practical reasoning. If a lion kills an antelope, the other antelopes have no consciousness of an injustice done to the victim and no thoughts of revenge. In general, there is a pattern of moral judgement and dialogue which is second nature to humans but which is foreign to a great many – perhaps all – other animals. If sometimes we think we discern this pattern, as in the social behaviour of baboons and chimpanzees, our attitude changes radically: and for very good reasons, as I shall later argue.

- Animals lack imagination. They can think about the actual and be anxious as to what the actual implies. (What is moving in that hedge?) But they cannot speculate about the possible, still less about the impossible.

- Animals lack the aesthetic sense: they enjoy the

world but not as an object of disinterested contemplation.

- In all sorts of ways, the passions of animals are circumscribed. They feel no indignation but only rage; they feel no remorse but only fear of the whip; they feel neither erotic love nor true sexual desire, only a mute attachment and a need for coupling.[7] To a great extent, as I have suggested, their emotional limitations are explained by their intellectual limitations. They are incapable of the thoughts on which the higher feelings depend.

- Animals are humourless and unmusical. Hyenas do not laugh nor do birds truly sing; it is we who hear laughter in the hyena's cackle and music in the song of the thrush.[8]

- Underlying all those, and many other, ways in which the animals fail to match our mental repertoire, there is the thing which, according to some philosophers, explains them all: namely, the fact that animals lack speech and are therefore deprived of all those thoughts, feelings and attitudes which depend upon speech for their expression. Of course, animals often emit noises and make gestures which *seem* like language. But, as I suggest in the section on language below, these noises and gestures lack the kind of organisation which makes human language into the remarkable and mind-transforming thing that it is.

When it is argued that animals are like us in one of

the above respects – animals like the higher apes who seem to have a sense of humour, or dolphins who seem to communicate their desires and to act in concert – the arguments tend to imply that these animals are like us in the other respects as well. It seems impossible to mount an argument for the view that the higher apes can laugh, which does not also attribute reasoning powers to them and maybe even language (or at least, the power to represent the world through symbols). It is an empirical question whether apes are like this or can be trained to be like this; but it is a philosophical question whether the capacities that I have described belong together or whether, on the contrary, they can be exemplified one by one. It is my considered view that they do indeed belong together and define a new and higher level of consciousness, for which 'reason' is a convenient shorthand.

SELF-CONSCIOUSNESS

What exactly do I mean by consciousness? To many people consciousness is the essence of the mental, the feature which makes the mind so important to us and the extinction of which is inherently regrettable in a way that the extinction of life (the life of a plant, say) is not. In asserting that animals are merely automata, Descartes was denying that they are conscious and a proof that Descartes was wrong will have far-reaching moral implications. If animals are conscious, then they feel things – for example, pain, fear and hunger – which it is intrinsically bad to feel. To inflict deliberately such experiences on an animal for no reason is either to treat an animal as a thing or else in some way to relish its suffering. And surely both those attitudes are immoral.

It is obvious that animals *are* conscious. This is proved by the fact that they are sometimes, but not all the time, *un*conscious. When asleep, anaesthetised or knocked out, a dog is not conscious, as it is when alertly running about the garden. To describe a dog as conscious is to imply that it is aware of its environment, responds to it, learns from it and is sentient. There is consciousness whenever behaviour must be explained in terms of mental activity. The dog has the kind of consciousness exhibited by its mental repertoire – which means that it is conscious as dogs are conscious but not as bees or humans are conscious.

We should be careful, therefore, to distinguish consciousness from self-consciousness. Human beings are aware of themselves and their own states of mind; they distinguish self from other and identify themselves in the first person. They knowingly refer to themselves as 'I', and are able to describe their own mental states for the benefit of others as well as themselves. This is what I mean by self-consciousness and it is a feature of our mental life which does not seem to be shared by the lower animals.

Someone might ask, 'How could you possibly know such a thing? Who are you to decide that my dog has no conception of himself, no consciousness of himself as distinct from his desires, beliefs and appetites?' The answer I propose is that it is redundant to assume otherwise. We can explain the dog's behaviour without recourse to such an hypothesis and therefore we have no grounds to affirm it.

We can justifiably attribute to animals only the mental repertoire that is needed to explain how they behave. The situation never arises which will compel us to describe a dog's behaviour in terms of a conscious distinction between self and other, or between the world from my point of view, and the world from yours. We can always make do with simpler assumptions – assumptions about beliefs and desires, in which the 'I' concept has no role.

Occasionally, we find ourselves doubting this; and in certain cases, notably those of apes, dolphins and elephants, our doubts have a persistent character which suggests that they may have a real foundation in what we observe. The interesting fact is not that we should be tempted to ascribe self-consciousness to some of the higher animals but that, whenever we do so, we are tempted to attribute to them rationality, linguistic or quasi-linguistic behaviour, humour, sympathy and even a moral sense. It seems that self-consciousness is another aspect of the higher level of mental activity, for which the term 'reason' has traditionally been reserved. It is an empirical question whether we are the only animals that exist at this higher level. I suspect that we are and that our uncertainty about the apes, the dolphin and the elephant stems from a commendable excess of sympathy which leads us to give them the benefit of the doubt. Their behaviour, occasionally and in an uncanny way, recalls the higher reaches of self-conscious emotion, and puzzles us for that very reason – as when we observe the coordinated dancing of the dolphins or the heart-rending mourning of the elephants.

LANGUAGE

Much of what I have said in the previous two sections will become clearer if we reflect on the way in which a creature's mental horizon is broadened by language – by the ability to represent the world through signs.

- Language expresses thoughts about absent things, about past and future things, about generalities, probabilities, possibilities and impossibilities. It emancipates thinking from the here and now and causes it to range freely over the actual, the possible and the impossible. We attribute beliefs to the lower animals; but without language, these beliefs seem to be confined to the here and now of perception.
- Language permits the construction of abstract arguments. It is the primary vehicle of reasoning and the means to adduce evidence for and against our beliefs and attitudes.
- Hence language permits new kinds of social relation, based in dialogue and conversation. It enables people to criticise and to justify each other's conduct, to provide reasons to each other and to

change each other's behaviour by persuasion. Thus arises the practice of reason-giving, immediate offshoots of which are inter-personal morality and the common law.

- Language expands the horizon of knowledge and contains the seeds of scientific inference. But it also expands the emotional horizons. No animal is able to fear some hypothetical event; to envy, esteem or cherish an individual whom it has never met; to feel jealous over its mate's past or apprehensive for its future.

- There are also emotions which are outside the repertoire of animals, since only a language-using creature could formulate the thoughts on which they depend. Thus indignation, remorse, gratitude, shame, pride and self-esteem all depend upon thoughts which are unavailable to creatures who cannot engage in reason-giving dialogue. For example, indignation is a response to injustice and injustice in turn a concept which only language users have. To cut a long story short, the higher emotions – those on which our lives as moral beings most critically depend – are available only to those who can live and think in symbols.

Much is controversial in philosophy. But I doubt that any philosopher who has studied the argument of Hegel's *Phenomenology of Spirit*, or that of Wittgenstein's *Philosophical Investigations*, would dissent from the view that self-consciousness and language emerge together, that both are *social* phenomena and that the Cartesian project – of discovering the essence of the mental in that which is private, inner and hidden from external view – is doomed to failure. Moreover, most philosophers would agree that language requires an elaborate social stage-setting – if Wittgenstein is right, nothing less than a shared form of life, based in a deep consensus, will suffice. It is possible that animals could be granted honorary membership of this form of life – like the unfortunate chimpanzee called Washoe, lifted from her natural innocence in order to compete with humans on terms which humans alone define.

But while there is a growing body of ethological evidence that animals communicate with each other and are able to pass complex information through signs, there is no evidence that they exhibit the kind of social organisation and self-reflective thinking required by language. Their signs are 'natural' signs: events from which information can be recovered but not symbolic representations of the thing described. Thus the levelled ears of a horse mean 'keep your distance' in the way that clouds mean rain and the dance of a bee indicates the direction of a food source in the way that the branches of a tree indicate the force of the wind. Of course there are some remarkable phenomena here, the dance of the bees being one of them.[9] But to describe these phenomena as linguistic systems, rather than natural signs, is to make a vast assumption about the intentions and thoughts of the animals who display them.

Suffice it to say that even the efforts of Washoe have failed to satisfy the philosophical sceptics. Crucial elements of symbolic behaviour – syntactic categories, logical connectives, the distinction between asserted and unasserted sentences – fail to emerge and in their absence it can reasonably be doubted that the ape has achieved true linguistic competence or risen to the level of self-reflective intention that is the distinguishing mark of *meaning* something. Maybe she has. But the missing components are precisely those which endow language with its ability to express thoughts beyond the present perception, to embed one thought within another, to entertain a thought without asserting it, to link thoughts in chains of hypothesis and argument and to multiply thoughts indefinitely, so as to present a comprehensive picture of reality as something independent of one's own interests and desires.

But there is no need to be dogmatic on this point. The real question is not this one, whether individual animals can be, as it were, coaxed from the state of nature into the fold of language users, nor even whether there might be whole species, such as the dolphin, which enjoy the full privileges of linguistic communication. The real question is whether the animals with whom we normally have to deal are language-using, self-conscious beings and, if not, whether this makes a vital difference to their moral status.

2

THE MORAL BEING

PERSONALITY

The facts to which I have been pointing could be described in another and more pregnant way, by saying that human beings are persons. The concept of the person, which we derive from Roman law, is fundamental to all our legal and moral thinking. It bears the meaning of Christian civilisation and of the ethic that has governed it, as well as the seeds of the Enlightenment vision which put Christianity in doubt. The masterly way in which this concept was lifted by Kant from the stream of social life and set upon a metaphysical pedestal should not distract us from its everyday employment as the concept through which human relations are brokered. Our relations to one another are not animal but personal and our rights and duties are those which only a person could have.

Human beings are, or believe themselves to be, free and their choices issue from rational decision making in accordance with both long-term and short-term interests. Although other animals are individuals, with thoughts, desires and characters that distinguish them, human beings are individuals in another and stronger sense, in that they are self-created beings. They *realise* themselves, through freely chosen projects and through an understanding of what they are and ought to be.

At the same time, human beings live in communities, upon which they depend not only for their specific ambitions and goals but also for the very language with which to describe and intend them. Hence there is a permanent and immovable possibility of conflict of a kind that does not occur in the animal kingdom. People depend on others and also need to be free from them. Freedom means conflict; community requires that conflict be peacefully resolved. Hence negotiation, compromise and agreement form the basis of all successful human communities.

The concept of the person should be seen in the light of this. It denotes potential members of a free community – a community in which the individual members can lead a life of their own. Persons live by negotiation and, through rational dialogue, create the space which their projects require. Such dialogue can proceed only on certain assumptions and these assumptions show us what persons really are.

- Both parties to the dialogue must be rational – that is, able to give and receive reasons for action and to recognise the distinction between good and bad reasons, between valid and invalid arguments, between justifications and mere excuses.

- Both parties must be free – that is, able to make choices, to act intentionally in pursuit of their goals and to take responsibility for the outcome.
- Both parties must desire the other's consent and be prepared to make concessions in order to obtain it.
- Both parties must be accepted as sovereign over matters which concern their very existence as freely choosing agents. Their life, safety and freedom must therefore be treated as inviolable and to threaten them is to change from dialogue to war.
- Each party must understand and accept obligations – for example, the obligation to honour an agreement.

Those assumptions can be expressed in another way, by saying that human communities are composed of persons, who have rights, responsibilities and duties and who endeavour to live by agreement with their fellows. If we do not recognise another's rights, then our relation to him is one of antagonism or war. If we do not feel bound by obligations, then we exist outside society and cannot rely on its protection. And in all negotiation we must recognise the freedom, rationality and sovereignty of the other, if the outcome is to be acceptable to the other and binding on both of us. All this is neatly summarised in the categorical imperative of Kant, which in its second formulation tells us that human beings are to be treated as ends and never as means only: in other words, their freedom and rights are to be respected and their agreement is to be sought in any conflict. We can see the Kantian 'moral law' as consisting precisely in those rules which rational beings would accept, when attempting to live by agreement.[1]

These rules compose the quasi-legal part of moral thinking and the concepts of right, obligation and personality gain their sense from them, just as the concepts of goal, foul and player gain their sense from the rules of football.

There is no doubt in my mind that animals do not form moral communities of the kind I have been describing. The concepts of right, duty, justice, personality, responsibility and so on have a sense for us largely because we deploy them in our negotiations and can invoke by their means the ground rules of social order which everyone, even our antagonists, must be seen to accept if they are to enjoy the protection of society.

PERSONS AND THE MORAL LAW

The ideas of freedom, responsibility, right and duty contain a tacit assumption that every player in the moral game counts for one and no player for more than one. By thinking in these terms, we acknowledge all persons as irreplaceable and self-sufficient members of the moral order. Their rights, duties and responsibilities are their own personal possessions.

Only they can renounce or fulfil them and only they can be held to account should their duties go unfulfilled. If this were not so, the 'moral law', as Kant calls it, would cease to fulfil its purpose of reconciling individuals in a society of strangers.

As Kant himself pointed out, the moral law has an absolute character. Rights cannot be arbitrarily overridden or weighed against the profit of ignoring them. Duties cannot be arbitrarily set aside or cancelled by the bad results of due obedience. I must respect your right, regardless of conflicting interests, since you alone can renounce or cancel it. That is the point of the concept – to provide an absolute barrier against invasion.[2] A right is an interest that is given special protection; it cannot be overridden or cancelled without the consent of the person who possesses it. By describing an interest as a right we lift it from the account of cost and benefit and place it in the sacred precinct of the self.

Likewise duty, if it is to exist at all, must have an absolute character. A duty can be set aside only when it ceases to be a duty – only when it has been fulfilled or cancelled. There can be conflicts of rights and conflicts of duties: but these conflicts are painful precisely because they cannot be resolved. We weigh rights against each other and give precedence to the one which we believe to be more serious – as when we take food that belongs to John in order to save the life of the starving Henry. Henry's right to help takes precedence over John's right to his property;

nevertheless John's right remains and John is wronged by the act which brings relief to Henry. The issues here are deep and complex. Suffice it to say that any attempt to deprive the concepts of right and duty of this absolute character would also deprive them of their utility. We should thereby rid ourselves of the supreme instrument which reason provides, whereby to live with others while respecting their freedom, their individuality and their sovereignty over the life that is theirs. That is what it means, in the last analysis, to treat persons as ends in themselves.

THE MORAL LIFE

The moral community is shaped by negotiation but depends upon many other factors for its life and vitality. In particular, it depends upon the affections of those who compose it and upon their ability to make spontaneous and self-sacrificing gestures for the good of others. A society ordered entirely by the moral law, in which rights, duties and justice take precedence over all interests and affections, would soon fall apart. For it would make no distinction between neighbours and strangers, between the alien and the friend. People need the safety promised by the moral law and by the habit of negotiation. But they also need something more: the nexus of affection and sympathy which binds them to their neighbours, which creates a common destiny and which leads people to share one another's sorrows and joys.

While we admire punctilious people who

perform all their duties and meticulously respect the rights of others, we cannot easily love them. But affection requires us to bend the rules, to set aside our rights in the interest of those we love, to do that which is beyond the call of duty and sometimes to dispense favours unjustly. And the same is true of sympathy – that generalised affection which spreads from the self in dwindling ripples across the world of others. Actions which spring from sympathy may resemble those commanded by the moral law; but they spring from another motive, one that is just as necessary to the moral life. The moral being is not merely the rule-governed person who plays the game of rights and duties but a creature of extended sympathies, motivated by love, admiration, shame and a host of other social emotions.

Hence we judge moral beings not only in terms of their actions but also in terms of their motives and characters. We know that social order is a precarious thing which cannot be sustained by law alone. Internal and external threats to it can be deterred only if people have the mettle to resist them – the force of character, the emotional equilibrium and the live human sympathies that will prompt them to persist in a cause, to make sacrifices and to commit themselves to others. This is the origin of the vital distinction that we make between vice and virtue.

The virtues that inspire our admiration are also the qualities which preserve society, whether from external threat or from internal decay: courage and resolution in the face of danger; loyalty and decency in private life; justice and charity in the public sphere. At different periods and in different conditions, the emphasis shifts – virtue is malleable and is shaped by material, spiritual and religious circumstances. Nevertheless, the constancy of the objects of human admiration is more significant than the local variations. The antique virtues of courage, prudence, wisdom, temperance and justice, amplified by Christian charity and pagan loyalty, still form the core idea of human excellence. It is these qualities that we admire, that we wish for in those we love and that we hope to be credited with ourselves.

Such qualities require a social setting. They are not solipsistic achievements like the muscles of the body-builder or the mortification of the anchorite. But this social setting is also an emotional setting and emotions are reactions not to the world as it is in itself but to the world as it is understood. The world is understood differently by people and animals. Our world, unlike theirs, contains rights, obligations and duties; it is a world of self-conscious subjects, in which events are divided into the free and the unfree, those which have reasons and those which are merely caused, those which stem from a rational subject and those which erupt in the stream of objects with no conscious design. Thinking of the world in this way, we respond to it with emotions that lie beyond the repertoire of other animals: indignation, resentment and envy; admiration, commitment and erotic love –

all of which involve the thought of the other as a free subject, with rights and duties and a self-conscious vision of his past and future. Only moral beings can feel these emotions and, in feeling them, they situate themselves in some way outside the natural order, standing back from it in judgement.

The sympathies of moral beings are also marked by this detachment from the natural order. A horse will run when the herd runs; a hound excited by a scent will communicate its excitement to its fellows; a partridge will throw herself between her brood and the fox that threatens them. The casual observer might see these actions as expressing sympathy – as animated by a feeling which in some way takes account of the feelings and interests of others. But they lack a crucial ingredient, which is *the thought of what the other is feeling*. In none of the cases that I have mentioned (and they form three archetypes of animal 'sympathy') do we need to invoke this very special thought in order to explain the animal's behaviour. It is a thought that is peculiar to moral beings, involving a recognition of the distinction between self and other, and of the other as *feeling what I might have felt*.

Likewise, maternal attachment, which greatly endears the mammals to us and which Kant believed to be the only real ground for extending to them the protection afforded by morality, should not mislead us into describing the relations between the non-human mother and her offspring in personal terms.

The relation of a mare to her foal is not an example of the I-Thou (*Ich-Du*) relation so poignantly explored by Martin Buber. The mare does not cherish her foal's life, personality or identity; does not stand vigil over its moral and psychological development; does not feel its pains and joys as her own; does not, when it is weaned, retain her burning attachment; does not, in later life, seek its constant affection. All such attitudes require a consciousness of self and other and of the relation between them, which is inherently absent from the mental repertoire of the non-human animals. Once weaned, the foal becomes another member of the herd, with no special relation to any other horse apart from the stallion-in-chief, while its mother rapidly forgets it.

Two of our sympathetic feelings are of great moral importance: pity towards those who suffer and pleasure in another's joy. And these two feelings lie at the root of our moral duties towards animals. Both feelings are held to be part of human virtue. Pitiless people and joyless people alike awaken our disapproval. True, Nietzsche mounted an assault on pity and on the 'herd morality' which he supposed to be contained in it. But most people remain unpersuaded, and rightly so. For pity and good cheer are complementary. You cannot rejoice in the joys of others without suffering their pains, and all pleasure requires the sympathy of others if it is to translate itself into joy. It seems to me, indeed, that there is something deeply contradictory in a philosophy that advocates joyful wisdom while slandering pity as the enemy of the higher life.

Indeed, whether we look at these emotions from the point of view of the individual or from that of society, we cannot fail to see them as indispensable parts of human goodness. Sympathy awakens sympathy: it draws us to itself and forms the bond of goodwill from which our social affections grow. Pitiless and joyless people are also affectionless; if they love, it is with a hard, dogged love that threatens to destroy what it cherishes. We avoid them as unnatural and also dangerous. The anger of a pitiless person is to be feared, as is the friendship of a joyless one. It is not the pitiless and the joyless who sustain the social order: on the contrary, they are parasites who depend on the overspill of sympathy which misleads us into forgiving them.

Nietzsche condemned pity for favouring the weak and the degenerate. In fact, pity is a necessary part of any society which is able to heal itself and to overcome disaster. It is indispensable in war as in peace, since it causes people to stand side by side with strangers in their shared misfortune and arouses them to anger and revenge against the common enemy.

Pity and sympathetic joy extend naturally to other species. I know that the dog with a broken leg is suffering, in something like the way that I would suffer. I know that the same dog, hunting on a lively scent, feels a joy that has its equivalent in me. Only a heartless person would feel no distress at the sight of such canine sufferings or no pleasure at the sight of such joys.

As I have already argued, it is an empirical question whether we humans are the only moral beings on earth. I am inclined to believe that we are indeed alone in this respect. I also believe that any proof that some other species had crossed the barrier into the moral realm would oblige us to treat its members as we treat each other. This would mean not only according rights to them, regarding their life, limb and freedom as inviolable, and accepting them as objects of the higher emotions. It would also mean imposing duties and responsibilities on them, reasoning with them and treating them as subject to the moral law. There are great benefits attached to the status of moral being, and also great burdens. Unless we are in a position to impose the burdens, the benefits make no sense – for they are benefits only to those who know how to use them, in other words, to those who regard themselves as bound by moral duties and answerable for their acts.

3

LIFE, DEATH, JOY AND SUFFERING

INDIVIDUALS

The argument that I have just given does not imply that all non-moral animals enjoy the same status from the point of view of the moral being. It is as right and natural to pity the gasping fish on the strand as the wounded stag at bay. But it is impossible for us to relate to fish as individuals – that is to say, with sentiments which single out the particular from the general. Yet, between the dog and the ape on the one hand, and the fish and the ant on the other, there is a host of animals which, while entertaining only a dim conception of the rival merits of individual humans, or while even looking on humans as we do on ants, as interchangeable parts of a collective nuisance, have a keen conception of the individuality of other members of their species. Horses, for instance, know who is who in the herd and will recognise and make a fuss of each other after months of separation. We, in turn, have no difficulty in treating them as individuals and in reserving our special favours for those which please us most. At the same time, their response to a human being is never truly individualising, as a dog's might be.

Peter Singer has considered the distinction between animals which do, and those which do not, exist as individuals.[1] The latter – among which he includes chickens and other birds – are, he suggests, inherently replaceable, partly at least because they have no conception of their own future existence and live 'in the present moment' alone. The painless death of one chicken is no loss in itself, provided another healthy bird is born in place of it: for our only criterion of good and evil in such a case is the total sum of pain and pleasure. The absence of one chicken's pleasure is made up for by the presence of another's. But the individuality of a dog or an elephant places a brake on such utilitarian reasoning, just as the individuality of the human being forbids us from sacrificing one person's happiness for the sake of another's greater good. There is a sense in which Jumbo the elephant is not replaceable by Dumbo; for his being and remaining Jumbo is fundamental to our concern for him. It is not possible to say, when Jumbo dies, that Dumbo can be brought in to replace him and Dumbo's pains and pleasures are not, therefore, to be weighed against the loss of Jumbo's.

A few observations must be made in response to this argument:

- The members of the higher species exist as individuals; that is to say, they contain within themselves the process which maintains them in being, with their parts sustained in mutual relation and inter-dependence. So long as the life of the dog persists, this leg and this eye are non-severable parts of a single system. The dog's life maintains the system in being through time in such a way as to determine that this is one enduring individual, whose individuality cannot be excised except by death from the book of the world.

- In that sense, however, ants, fish and chickens are all genuine individuals. They too are members of natural kinds, individual systems which come into being and pass away in accordance with the laws of the species. Of course, there are odd individuals: one and the same creature is now a caterpillar, now a butterfly; now a tadpole, now a frog (though never a prince). But this only shows how immovable is the distinction between numerical and qualitative identity: for here are individuals which seem to change in every qualitative respect, while remaining numerically the same.

- Grafted on to the metaphysical idea of the individual, however, is another concept, according to which individuality is a kind of achievement. In an important sense, the individual ant has no history; it is unmarked by experience and remains the same at death as it was at birth – a machine-like soldier, indistinguishable in its knowledge and responses from any other member of its kind. The more a creature is able to learn from and adapt to its environment, the more it acquires a character that distinguishes it from other members of its species and the more we can work on it, so as to imprint on its rude behaviour a simulacrum of our own response. As we ascend the levels of mental activity, therefore, we find ourselves increasingly able to attribute character, history and emotional and intellectual development to the animals, to the point where some of them – notably those whom we can train to react selectively to humans – acquire an individuality which makes the gift of a proper name appropriate. And the high point is reached with those animals like dogs, which not only have names but also respond to names as their own.

- When we come to the rational level of mental life, however, a wholly new kind of individuality emerges. Unlike the lower animals, rational beings are conscious of their own individuality and refer to themselves in the first person. Their individuality is not a passive thing, attributed by others; it is something that they assert against the world. They make choices, take individual responsibility for the outcome and possess rights and duties as individuals. In short, there is a special kind of individuality which comes with the status of moral being and which cannot be reduced to the individuality exemplified by a cat or a dog.

• The individuality of the moral agent exists also as a constraint upon treatment by others. The human individual is not replaceable by another, has no equivalent, is not a means to an end or subject to another's uses. Around the moral being, therefore, a sovereign territory exists, which cannot be entered without permission. This fact is enshrined in our concept of a right, in the idea of the person and in the moral law and its prohibitions. People cannot be owned, enslaved or violated; they cannot be bent to another's purpose except with their rational consent; to approach them with love or desire requires elaborate courtship, so that the outcome will be freely chosen. All these facts are blindingly obvious to anyone who has a passing acquaintance with art and literature, whether or not they are captured by Kant's philosophical account of them.

There are those who believe that animals, too, are to be treated 'as ends in themselves'. 'In my morality,' writes Stephen Clark, 'all creatures with feelings and wishes should be thought of as ends-in-themselves, and not merely as means.'[2] But I find no cogent explanation of what this could mean, apart from the fact that animals are not to be treated as things, since to do so is to disregard their capacity for suffering.

From those observations we may conclude that the individuality of animals offers us no guidance in our moral dealings with them. For it is individuality of the wrong kind. If animals possessed the self-consciousness and autonomy of the moral being, then they would also have rights and duties. But animals do not achieve individuality of this kind. Nor does the average animal lover think otherwise. For the moral being cannot be treated as a pet, cannot be trained, domesticated or coddled without consent. He cannot be kept, as dogs and cats are kept, for our purposes, not even for the purpose of companionship, unless that companionship is freely and knowingly bestowed. While we soon come to love our pets, we allow them no real choice in the matter and get rid of them without compunction if they return our advances with bites and scratches and snarls.

When we become attached to an animal, we see it as an individual and as a result we lift it from its species being, set it down in our midst and endow it with an honorary personality, in which we see as in a mirror the shining face of our own benevolence. In doing this thing to an animal we undertake an obligation towards it. For we remove from it all ability to fend for itself. But this obligation does not convert the animal into a moral being. It is part of the pathos of a pet that it stands always on the edge of the moral dialogue, staring from beyond an impassable barrier at the life which is now everything to it and yet which it cannot comprehend.

LIFE, DEATH AND NATURE

Underlying our thoughts about individuality is the idea that some animals at least have a life of their own and that the loss of this life is for them a calamity.[3] Sympathy and fellow-feeling prompt us to share in the fear with which such animals encounter death and to look on their death as something intrinsically evil, to be put off until the day when death is the least of impending evils.

The distinctions between the various levels of mental life are relevant here. Insects, and other animals which lack the ability to learn, contain no growing store of knowledge and affections. Nothing changes in their motivation and no attachment to this world is evinced in their behaviour that is not also evinced by a plant or a virus. True, they shun the more obvious dangers – but only in the mechanical way required by their mental 'software'. It is hard to think of these animals as having 'a life of their own'; and hard to think of their death as an evil greater than the death of a plant. Although I instinctively recoil from stepping on the spider who lies in my path, so do I instinctively recoil from stepping on a forget-me-not. Yet neither of those responses expresses the fellow-feeling that forbids me to step on a rabbit or a mouse.

An animal that learns, that forms attachments, that gradually develops both cognitively and emotionally, seems to attach itself to life in a way that bears comparison with our own endeavours. Such an animal can grow into its world, make a niche for itself in the thoughts and emotions of those who live with it, gain a hold on our affections and prompt us to take sides with it in the universal struggle against extinction. Its life is 'its own' and its death a true catastrophe.

Even so, we do not look on the death of such an animal as we should look on the death of a person. This is shown by a peculiar fact: as soon as we decide that the balance of pain over pleasure has shifted decisively in favour of pain, we feel no compunction in 'putting the animal out of its misery' – and therefore out of ours. We even speak, in such a case, of 'humane' killing: meaning that death is here a kindness and one that we may be duty-bound to provide.

Now there are people who think of human beings in such a way. But nobody would dream of putting a sick man 'out of his misery' without first securing his own most fervent and considered consent – indeed, without making sure that he himself initiates the process and relieves us of the responsibility that would otherwise attach to killing him. Simply put, the death of a person is an evil of another order from the evil of pain and cannot be weighed against it. To enter into calculations of the kind that motivate us when we have a lame horse 'destroyed' would be to show a peculiar kind of moral corruption – the corruption involved when a moral being is treated as just another part of the natural order.

Moreover, with the death of a self-conscious

creature something else is removed besides life: namely, the consciousness of life as *mine*. In this thought, so difficult to unravel, is contained the mystery and tragedy of our condition.

We should also note that nature is not, in general, kind to the animals. Animals in the wild have to work continuously to feed themselves, pass long days of hunger and discomfort, are in constant fear of predators and find comfort and safety only in those first few months of mammalian succour, shielded from the reality which soon will burst upon them. The lucky ones will die in the jaws of something larger than themselves – it takes only a few seconds for a lion to smother an antelope or for a terrier to decapitate a rat. Far less lucky are the predators themselves, whose death is a lingering and painful affair when old age, disease or injury removes their capacity to feed themselves. Less fortunate still are those who are killed by creatures smaller than themselves: by the worms which gnaw, the maggots which suck and the bacteria which inflame their helpless bodies. From all these calamities animals gain relief and protection when we decide to offer it. But this offer is not made without a motive and we should work to keep that motive alive. By eating meat, drinking milk, wearing leather and furs, even by shooting and angling, we may, if circumstances are right, reinforce the desire to alleviate the unkindnesses of nature. And if it be said that we do so only to replace them with unkindnesses of our own, let it also be said that there is a moderation and control in human unkindness of which nature knows nothing.

SUFFERING

Many have followed Jeremy Bentham, the founding father of utilitarianism, in regarding animals as included in the moral equation, purely on account of their feelings: 'the question is not can they reason? Nor, can they talk? But, can they suffer?'⁴ That this is too simple an approach to the problem should by now be obvious: while it may have the result (agreeable to utilitarians) of reducing moral questions to a single calculation, it does so only at the cost of dismissing the moral law and all that is contained in it. In other words, it ignores the most fundamental function of moral thinking, which is to establish a community founded on negotiation and consent.

Nevertheless, it is hard to deny that suffering is morally significant, that it is experienced by animals and that it is wrong to inflict it deliberately without cause. Why it is wrong is a question that I consider below. Before doing so it is important to make one or two observations about the notion of suffering itself.

Firstly, the sufferings of a self-conscious being have an added dimension. We do not only feel pain, we anticipate it, rehearse it and accompany it with frightening thoughts of its cause. Unlike the lower animals, we know pain as the sign of a deep disorder and while we shun pain as they do, we are also aware of its terrible significance. A fox hit by a car drags its broken leg painfully behind it, but does not know that this broken leg means death. A man with a broken leg knows that he must seek help and, if help is out of the question, that he must die in agony.

Secondly, we should not think that all pain is an evil or that it is always wrong to inflict it. A just punishment is painful: but it is also right both to suffer and to inflict this pain, even if no other benefit proceeds from doing so. It is one of the well-known paradoxes of utilitarianism that it cannot justify this conclusion; nevertheless, it is a conclusion towards which our moral intuitions naturally incline us and one in which we should see the mark of the moral law. Punishment, it seems to me, is a necessary feature of any community which recognises the freedom and responsibility of those who compose it.

Thirdly, to focus exclusively on suffering is to present a caricature of moral thought. As I shall argue, morality stems from at least four sources and only one of these makes suffering into the principal fact. Those who see no further than suffering blind themselves to much that is worthwhile. Just as human beings can develop as persons only through a measure of pain, so do animals enjoy the fullness of animal life only if they are exposed to the risk of suffering. To remove that risk is easy, but the result is not a life that an animal should lead.

Fourthly, we should note how selective human beings are, and must be, in their attitude to the sufferings of other species. Every turn of the fork in the garden and every footstep along a country road brings pain to crawling creatures. But we can avoid this pain only by so amending our lives as to destroy our most precious encounters with nature. Should we do this? Should we be so solicitous of those whose sufferings we cause as to go on tip-toe through life, curtailing all our ventures lest they weigh down the balance of woe? To answer 'yes' to this question is, I believe, to lose sight of what morality is for, and therefore to destroy the basis of one's moral judgement.

4

THE MORAL MARGIN

THE BEHAVIOURAL CONTINUUM

It will be said that *natura non fecit saltus* – that nature makes no leaps – and therefore that between the moral being and the cognitive animal there ought to be a continuum, with a grey area in which it simply cannot be determined whether rights, duties and so on are to be imputed on the basis of what we observe. The existence of this continuum is precisely what motivates people who advocate animal 'rights' or who recommend at least that we extend to animals the protection offered by the moral law. To behave in any other way is to make an absolute division, where in fact there is only a gradual transition and a difference of degree.[1]

Two points should be made in answer to this argument. First, the distinguishing features of the moral being – including rationality and self-consciousness – belong to another *system* of behaviour from that which characterises the merely cognitive animal. The transition from the one behavioural system to the other is as absolute a transition as that from vegetable to sentient life, or that from sentience to appetite. This is confirmed by all the other concepts which seem to pile in irresistibly behind the ideas of rationality and personhood – concepts which suggest a distinct form of mental life, unknown to the lower animals.

The second point is this. It is true that we arrive at the rational from the merely animal by the route of behaviour, and that there are degrees of complexity both before and after the transition. But we are dealing here, in Hegel's phrase, with a 'transition from quantity to quality'. Something wholly new emerges as a result of a process which merely adapts what is old. An analogy may help to understand the point. An array of dots on a canvas may look like an array of dots and nothing more. But suddenly, with the addition of just one more dot, a face appears. And this face has a character, a meaning and an identity which no array of dots could ever have. In a similar way, at a certain level of complexity, the behaviour of an animal becomes the expression of a self-conscious person. And this transition is well likened to the emergence of a face, a look, a gaze. Another subject now stands before me, seeing me, not as an animal sees me, but I to I.

MARGINAL HUMANS

But this brings me to a vexed question, much emphasised by Regan and Singer, the question of 'marginal humans', as Regan describes them. Even if we grant a distinction between moral beings and other animals, and recognise the importance of rationality, self-consciousness and moral dialogue in defining it, we must admit that many human beings do not lie on the moral side of the dividing line. For example, infants are *not yet* members of the moral community; senile and brain-damaged people are *no longer* members; congenital idiots *never will be* members. Are we to say that they have no rights? Or are we to say that, since they differ in no fundamental respect from animals, that we ought in consistency to treat other animals as we treat these 'marginal' humans? Whichever line we take, the hope of making an absolute moral distinction between human and animal life collapses.

It seems to me that we should clearly distinguish the case of 'pre-moral' infants, from those of the 'post-moral' and 'non-moral' human adults. The former are *potential* moral beings, who will naturally develop, in the conditions of society, into full members of the moral community. Our attitude towards them depends on this fact; and indeed, it is only because we look on them as incipiently rational that we eventually elicit the behaviour that justifies our treatment. Just as an acorn is, by its nature, the seed of an oak tree, so is an infant, by its nature, a potential rational being. And it is only by treating it as such that we enable it to realise this potential and so to become what it essentially is.

The other cases of 'marginal humans' are more problematic. And this is instinctively recognised by all who have to deal with them. Infanticide is an inexcusable crime; but the killing of a human vegetable, however much we shrink from it, may often strike us as understandable, even excusable. Although the law may treat this act as murder, we ourselves, and especially those upon whom the burden falls to protect and nurture this unfortunate creature, will seldom see it in such a light. On the other hand, to imagine that we can simply dispose of mental cripples is to display not only a callousness towards the individual, but also a cold and calculating attitude to the human species and the human form. It is part of human virtue to acknowledge human life as sacrosanct, to recoil from treating other humans, however hopeless their life may seem to us, as merely disposable and to look for the signs of personality wherever the human eye seems able to meet and return our gaze. This is not part of virtue only; it is a sign of piety. And, as I shall argue in the next chapter, virtue and piety are cornerstones of moral thinking.

There is a further point to be made. Our world makes sense to us because we divide it into kinds, distinguishing animals and plants by species and instantly recognising the individual as an example of the universal. This recognitional expertise is essential to survival and especially to the survival of the hunter-gatherer.[2] And it is essential also to the moral life. I relate to you as a human being and accord to you the privileges attached to the kind. It is in the nature of human beings that, in normal conditions, they become members of a moral community, governed by duty and protected by rights. Abnormality in this respect does not cancel membership. It merely compels us to adjust our response. Infants and imbeciles belong to the same kind as you or me: the kind whose normal instances are also moral beings. It is this that causes us to extend to them the shield that we consciously extend to each other and which is built collectively through our moral dialogue.

It is not just that dogs and bears do not belong to the moral community. They have no potential for membership. The are not *the kind of thing* that can settle disputes, that can exert sovereignty over its life and respect the sovereignty of others, that can respond to the call of duty or take responsibility on a matter of trust. Moreover, it should be noted that we do not accord to infants and imbeciles the same rights as we accord to normal adults: in many of our dealings with them we assume the right to by-pass their consent. Their disabilities have moral consequences. And although infants cause us no difficulties, since we curtail their rights only in order to enhance them, imbeciles cause us real moral problems.

Much more needs to be said about these difficult cases; for our purposes it is enough, however, to recognise that the difficulty arises not because we make no distinction between moral beings and animals, but precisely because we do make such a distinction, and on very good grounds. It is precisely this that lands us with such an intractable problem, when our instinctive reverence for human beings is thwarted by their inability to respond to it. Our difficulties over 'marginal humans' do not cast doubt on the moral distinction between people and animals; on the contrary, they confirm it.

5

THE ROOTS
OF MORAL
THINKING

I shall now sketch an account of moral judgement which will show its rational basis and its place in the lives of moral beings. Although this is one of the most controversial of all areas in philosophy, it is possible again to proceed by making minimal assumptions and confining the more intractable controversies to corners where they can do no damage.

UTILITARIANISM

The question of animals would be easily resolved were we to adopt an old-fashioned utilitarian morality of the kind proposed by Bentham and then qualified out of existence by John Stuart Mill. If we thought that moral thinking had only one purpose, which is to maximise the balance of pleasure over pain, then it would seem irrational not to consider the animals, who feel both these things, as on a par with humans. But it was precisely the inability of utilitarianism to explain the distinction between animals and people which led to its rejection. We cannot kill a sick old man to feed a swarm of hungry rats, great as the net balance of pleasure over pain might be. But we can kill a healthy bullock to feed a sick old man – and in certain circumstances we must do so, if we are not to do wrong. These and related considerations remind us that, while the pleasures and pains of animals may very well enter our moral calculations, something more is at stake than the mere sum of them.

Utilitarianism has encountered objections judged to be unanswerable by all but its staunchest advocates. A brief summary will serve to remind us of what is at stake in our moral reasoning.

- *Happiness:* utilitarianism is forced to replace the ancient goal of morality – happiness – with a measurable substitute – usually the scale of pleasure and pain, though appeal may sometimes be made to the econometric concept of 'revealed preference'. But happiness is peculiar to rational beings. It involves a self-reflexive judgement, an awareness of, and contentment with, one's condition. It may be true, as Aristotle argued, that we all have reason to aim at happiness. But this gives us no means for calculating the answers to moral questions, since the happiness of one person cannot be placed on a scale that will measure it against the happiness of another. In any case, animals are never happy as we are – merely pleased, comfortable and well.

- *Justice:* if our only concern is the balance of pleasure over pain, then injustice ceases to be an obstacle. If the cause of pleasure is served by executing an innocent person, then that is the right thing to do. There is an extensive utilitarian literature devoted to overcoming this difficulty, through revised and sophisticated forms of the original utilitarian principle. But, like many people who have studied this literature, I believe that it amounts to first aid, not cure. In effect, utilitarianism involves setting aside the moral law, with its concept of rights and duties, and taking a purely calculating approach to practical questions.

- *Blame:* Lenin, Stalin and Hitler all justified their actions in utilitarian terms, speaking of the regrettable necessity of doing away with whole classes and races in order to secure the long-term good of society. A sincere utilitarian never does wrong, he merely makes mistakes. At the same time, no one is in a position to accuse him, for who knows what the real long-term effect of his actions might be? Most of us would regard a moral philosophy which makes it impossible to pass final judgement on Hitler and Stalin as a kind of sick joke.

- *Responsibility:* for similar reasons, utilitarianism makes nonsense of responsibility. If I spend my money on my child's education, I make a contri- bution to the sum of human happiness. But the same amount of money, spent on the children of strangers in another continent, goes much further. The utilitarian must therefore say that I should spend my money on those foreign children. Yet we all recognise that our duties are circumscribed by our personal ties.

The utilitarian recognises no moral absolutes, no action which could not be justified by 'further and better particulars', no injustice which might not also be the right thing to do. He is obsessed with a particular paradigm of rationality – 'instrumental reasoning', or the calculation of means to a single and measurable end. For the utilitarian there is something irrational in the refusal to reason further; if morality is to be based in reason, then all questions are open until reasoning brings them to a close. His morality is really a species of economics, in which profit and loss have been replaced by pleasure and pain, and in which no moral problems occur which could not be solved by a competent accountant. It is nearer the truth, I maintain, to think of morality as setting the *limits* to economic reasoning, rather than being a species of it. Moral principles tell us precisely that we must go no further along the path of calculation and that the desire to do so is a kind of corruption. That this corruption is the ruling vice of modern societies gives us no grounds for condoning it.

THE MORAL LAW
Look back now at the account of the rational agent

given earlier and you will find an altogether different picture. Rational agents in my description are also moral beings, with a distinctive motivation and a distinctive emotional life. Their relations with other rational agents are mediated by ideas of right and obligation, and rights cannot be overridden by calculation, nor obligations extinguished by it. On this view, the rational agent is precisely one who recognises certain issues as closed – the rational being is one who sometimes refuses to reason.

The categorical imperative, which treats all persons as sovereign, forbids us to override the rights of others and holds us to our duties. And surely, this corresponds to our ordinary intuitions as to what moral thinking really is and why it is important.

SYMPATHY

Yet reason alone is not a motive to action. Moral beings act on principle and respect the rights of others not because reason points them in this direction but because they are social creatures, able to see the other's point of view, brought up to restrain their passions, to cultivate the virtues and to sympathise with their fellow human beings. Their sympathies propel them in the direction of Kant's imperative but their sympathies are not the product of reason alone. Indeed, their sympathies also open the mind and the heart to favouritism, mercy and white lies and to bending the rules in favour of those who do not have the strength or the good fortune that would make it easy to obey them.

To cut a long story short: it seems to me that the moral law – the law which governs negotiation between persons – must have an absolute component. Otherwise rights and duties count for nothing. At the same time, however, the moral being, who acknowledges this law, is shaped by sympathy and its special form of charity, both of which are necessary if the law is really to be a motive. The ethic of sympathy must therefore be acknowledged in any moral thinking that could be recommended to rational beings. Many of our most troubling moral conflicts stem from the fact that, while sympathy provides the underlying motive to obey the moral law, it may also, in the individual case, prompt our disobedience. The very same feelings that implant in me the absolute interdiction against killing an innocent human being may tempt me, when confronted by the unbearable suffering of a hopeless invalid who begs to be relieved of his torment, to disobey. How we ought to respond to such dilemmas is a matter that I touch on in the next chapter.

VIRTUE

Dilemmas remind us of the danger of an ethic founded in sympathy alone. For sympathies can be swayed; they impart a warm sense of self-approval to every action that they cause, regardless of its moral worth, and a person who lives by sympathy may undermine the moral order as effectively as the one who lives by crime. The sympathies of crowds are notoriously fickle and dangerous; those of individuals scarcely less so. Only in the virtuous character – the character schooled in self-denial – does sympathy feed the moral sense. Many of our deepest moral motives stem from our appreciation of this fact. The coward, the liar, the rake and the cheat disgust us: their very gestures set our teeth on edge. The brave, just, temperate and self-sacrificing person does not merely enlist our support and goodwill, but stands forth as an ideal and a model. Stories of vice and virtue therefore form a large part of moral education.

The principal aim of this education is not to teach the moral law – which in general teaches itself – but to induce the kind of character that *obeys* the law, even when its own interests and desires point in another direction.

What qualities should such a character have? The traditional 'cardinal' virtues, of courage, justice, prudence, wisdom and temperance have retained their place at the centre of moral thinking – and rightly so. Christian charity and pagan loyalty are of equal importance. And it is part of charity to pity needless suffering, to shrink from causing it and to offer help and comfort when confronted by its victim. Virtue and vice are seamless: justice that is selective towards its beneficiary is not justice but favouritism; kindness that specialises in the sufferings of a particular group, class or species, is not kindness. The concept of virtue, therefore, makes a substantial contribution to the question of how we should treat animals.

It compels us to distinguish virtuous and vicious attitudes towards other creatures, regardless of whether those creatures are moral beings like us.

PIETY

But there is a fourth component in moral thought which must be mentioned – the component which I shall call piety. Because 'piety' is a provocative word, I must add that I wish to divest it of its specifically Christian connotations in order to return it to something like the use that it had in late antiquity, when it expressed an idea of permanent validity in moral thinking.

For the Romans, belief in the gods and their fantastic stories was less important than the punctilious respect towards sacred things. *Pietas* requires that we honour our parents and ancestors, the household deities, the laws and the civil order, that we keep the appointed festivals and public ceremonies – and all this out of a sense of the sacred given-ness of these things, which are not our invention and to which we owe an unfathomable debt of gratitude.

It seems to me that, beneath all moral sentiment, there lies a deep layer of pious feeling. It is a feeling which does not depend explicitly on religious belief and which no moral being can really escape, however little it may be overtly acknowledged. Kantians and utilitarians may regard pious feelings as the mere residue of moral thinking; but they are not a residue at all. Put in simple terms, piety means the deep down recognition of our frailty and dependence, the acknowledgement that the burden we inherit cannot be sustained unaided, the disposition to give thanks for our existence and reverence to the world on which we depend and the sense of the unfathomable mystery which surrounds our coming to be and our passing away. All these feelings come together in our humility before the works of nature and this humility is the fertile soil in which the seeds of morality are planted. The three forms of moral life that I have described – respect for persons, the pursuit of virtue and natural sympathy – all depend, in the last analysis, on piety. For piety instils the readiness to be guided and instructed, and the knowledge of our own littleness which make the gift of moral conduct – whereby we are lifted from our solitude – so obviously desirable.

Piety is rational in the sense that we all have reason to feel it. Nevertheless, piety is not, in any clear sense, *amenable to reason*. Indeed, it marks out another place where reasoning comes to an end. The same is true, it seems to me, of many moral attitudes and feelings: while it is supremely rational to possess them, they are not themselves amenable to reason, and the attempt to make them so produces the kind of ludicrous caricature of morality that we witness in utilitarianism.

This does not mean that we must simply accept one another's prejudices. On the contrary, morality fails its purpose if people cannot reach agreement and amend their views and feelings in the light of experience, with a view to accommodating others. It means, rather, that we should not expect a 'decision procedure' which will settle moral questions finally and unambiguously. In these areas, the task of reason is to clarify our intuitions, to recognise the nature and extent of our commitments and to search for the points of agreement which will provide a fulcrum on which our prejudices may be turned.

Since the Enlightenment, moral thought has shied away from piety and invested its greatest energy in those abstract legal ideas associated with the respect for persons. This has happened for many reasons and it is not the purpose of this work to examine them. But it is worth observing that the moral question about animals, which comes vividly to the fore with our loss of religious confidence and in that sense owes some of its power to the decline of traditional pieties, represents at the same time, for many people, a return to piety. For such people we must regain the attitude towards the natural world which once prevailed, in which the species were regarded as sacred and humanity had not yet asserted absolute sovereignty, rather than humble trusteeship, over the works of nature. It is not unreasonable to believe that modern civilisation has destroyed a precious part of the human soul in its arrogant assertion of a right to control and exploit the world's resources. Industrialisation, spoliation, over-production and the destruction of the environment all spring from a single source, which is the loss of piety. In the face of this, the consciousness of animals and their welfare not only invokes our lost edenic innocence but also reminds us of another and more sacred order, more delicate and more beautiful than the one that we, with our cold rationality, have established.

I believe that we must respect the feeling of piety. However deep it may be concealed within our psyche, it is by no means a redundant part of the moral consciousness but, on the contrary, the source of our most valuable social emotions. It is piety, and not reason, that implants in us the respect for the world, for its past and its future, and that impedes us from pillaging all we can before the light of consciousness fails in us.

It is piety, too, which causes us to exalt the human form in life and art. Perhaps there are moral beings who are not humans: angels, devils and divinities, if they exist. But we have no direct experience of them. We have no clear image of morality save the image of the human form; such doubts as we feel about the elephant, the dolphin and the chimpanzee are too insecure to revise the overwhelming authority, for us, of the human face and gesture:

> For Mercy has a human heart,
> Pity a human face,
> And Love the human form divine,
> And Peace, the human dress.

Blake's words flow from the fount of reverence that

springs in all of us and causes us not merely to cherish the works of unblemished nature, but to look on the human being as somehow exalted above them. I do not mean that all humans are admirable or lovable: far from it. But they are all in some way untouchable. An air of sacred prohibition surrounds humanity, since the 'human form divine' is our only image of the moral being – the being who stands above nature, in an attitude of judgement. This is the true reason why we cannot look on the 'marginal humans' discussed in the last chapter in the same way as we look on animals. And although we cannot justify the distinction case by case, we can justify the feeling from which it flows. The very same reverence which leads us to favour animal life, leads us to favour human life yet more.

6

THE RATIONAL BASIS OF MORAL JUDGEMENT

How should we reason about moral questions? It follows from the above account of the sources of moral sentiment that there will be four separate sources of moral argument: personality, with its associated moral law; the ethic of virtue; sympathy and, finally, piety. Most of our moral difficulties and 'hard cases' derive from the areas where these four kinds of thinking deliver conflicting results.

THE MORAL LAW

We do not need to accept Kant's sublime derivation of the categorical imperative in order to recognise that human beings tend spontaneously to agree about the morality of inter-personal relations. As soon as we set our own interests aside and look on human relations with the eye of the impartial judge, we find ourselves agreeing over the rights and wrongs in any conflict. Whatever their philosophical basis, the following principles of practical reasoning are accepted by all reasonable people:

- the principle of moral equality, which means that considerations which justify or impugn one person will, in identical circumstances, justify or impugn another
- rights are to be respected
- obligations are to be fulfilled
- agreements are to be honoured
- disputes are to be settled by rational argument and not by force
- persons who do not respect the rights of others forfeit rights of their own.

For a very long time, philosophers have written of such principles as defining the 'natural law' – the law which lies above all actual legal systems and provides the test of their validity. Some of the principles have been explicitly incorporated into international law – notably the fourth. They provide us with the calculus of rights and duties with which our day-to-day relations with strangers must be conducted, if we are to live by negotiation and not by force or fraud.

We should see the above principles as 'procedural' rather than 'substantive'. They do not tell us what our rights and duties are, but only what it means to describe an interest as a right, and a decision as a duty. Nevertheless, once this procedure is in place – once human beings are in the habit of settling their disputes by an assignment of rights, responsibilities and duties – it cannot be an open question what our rights and duties are. We will be constrained to settle questions in a manner on which all can agree, and – just as in the common law, which is no more than an extended application of this kind of reasoning – we will tend to agree, just as long as we look on all conflict as though it were the conflict of others, and observe it with the eye of an impartial judge.

VIRTUE

Although rational beings, adopting the standpoint of the impartial judge, will tend to endorse the principles given above, it does not follow that they will act on them when their interests tend in some other direction. But there are settled dispositions of character which will ensure that people overcome the temptations posed by greed, self-interest and fear. It is reasonable to admire and cultivate these dispositions therefore, which owe their reasonableness to the same considerations as justify the moral law. Only just people will act on the impartial verdict when their own interests conflict with it; only courageous people will uphold the moral law when others jeer at it; only temperate people will place rights and duties above the call of appetite. And so on. In short, the traditional virtues provide a source of moral reasoning which endorses the calculus of rights and duties. Whatever reasons we have for accepting the moral law, they are reasons for cultivating the virtues.

SYMPATHY

To the traditional virtues, which prepare us for membership of a moral community, we must add the wider and more flexible virtues which stem from sympathy. Christian charity (*caritas*, or fellow-feeling) is pre-eminent among these wider virtues. Philosophically speaking, charity is the disposition to put yourself in another's shoes and to be motivated on his behalf.

This, too, is a reasonable motive, for without it the moral community would be deprived of its most vital source of strength, and the individual of the most important reward attached to membership – the pleasure of giving and receiving in reciprocal concern.

It is here, however, that the potential clash arises between utilitarian ways of thinking and the calculus of rights. The charitable instinct identifies with joy and suffering wherever it finds them and, faced with the bewildering extent of these emotions, finds itself compelled to reason in a utilitarian way. Charity hopes to maximise joy and minimise suffering in general just as all people spontaneously act to maximise joy and minimise suffering in themselves. To think in this way, however, is to enter into inevitable conflict with the more sophisticated pattern of reasoning that underpins the moral community. I cannot treat persons as the subject-matter of a utilitarian calculation. I cannot inflict deliberate pain on John in order to relieve the twofold suffering of Elizabeth and Mary, without consulting the rights and duties of the parties.

We ascribe rights to people precisely because their freedom and their membership of the moral community forbid us from invading their space.

In short, even if utilitarian reasoning is a natural expression of the sympathy on which the moral life depends, reason demands that it be applied only selectively and within the framework established by the moral law. Questions of right, duty and responsibility must be settled first; only then does the utilitarian calculus apply. A few examples will make this clear. Suppose John is suffering from kidney failure, and only one other person, Henry, is of the same blood group. With one of Henry's kidneys, John could lead a healthy and normal life while Henry's life would not be significantly impaired. This utilitarian calculation is entirely irrelevant when faced with the question whether we ought to compel Henry to release one of his kidneys. For that is something we have no right to do, and all reasoning stops once this moral truth is recognised.

Suppose Elizabeth and Jane are both suffering from a rare disease, and William, Jane's husband, has obtained at great expense a quantity of the only drug that will cure it. By administering the whole quantity to Jane he ensures a 90 per cent chance of her survival; by dividing it between Jane and Elizabeth, he will provide a 60 per cent chance of recovery to both. Again, the utilitarian calculation, which might seem to favour division, is irrelevant. For William has a special responsibility towards his wife, which must be discharged before the welfare of any stranger can be taken into account.

Suppose that Alfred is driving a lorry, the maintenance of which he is not responsible for, and discovers that the brakes have failed. If he swerves to the right he kills a man at a bus stop; if he takes no action he will run down two pedestrians at a crossing, while if he swerves to the left he will drive into a crowd of children. Here, surely, the utilitarian calculus applies and Alfred would be blamed for not applying it. By swerving to the right he absolves himself of all responsibility for the death of the victim, while at the same time minimising the human cost of the disaster. The brake failure is not an action of Alfred's, but a misfortune that afflicts him. His principal duty, in such a case, is to minimise the suffering that results from it.

Such examples show the true goal of utilitarian thinking, which is not to replace or compete with the moral law, but to guide us when the moral law is silent and when only sympathy speaks. Hence utilitarian reasoning is of the first importance in our dealings with animals – in particular with those animals to which we have no special duty of care.

We should not imagine, however, that the utilitarian calculus could ever achieve the mathematical precision which Bentham and his followers have wished for. There is no formula for measuring the value of a life, the seriousness of a creature's suffering or the extent of its happiness or joy. To reason in a utilitarian way is to reason as Alfred does in my example: through numbers when these are suggested (as here, where Alfred must count the numbers of threatened lives); but otherwise through asking whether 'things in general would be better if . . .'. Those who wish to reduce such reasoning to an econometric calculation rid the moral question of its distinctive character, and replace it with questions of another kind – questions concerning 'preference orderings', 'optimising' and 'satisficing' solutions, and rational choice under conditions of risk and uncertainty. By shaping the moral question so that it can be fed into the machinery of economics, we do not solve it. On the contrary, we put a fantasy problem for experts in place of the painful reality of moral choice.

If the answer to moral questions were really to be found in decision theory, then most people would be unable to discover it. In which case morality would lose its function as a guide to life, offered to all of us by the fact of reasoned dialogue.

PIETY

Finally, there is the sphere of piety. As I have argued, piety is rational, but not amenable to reason. People who try to rationalise their pieties completely have in a sense already lost them. The best we can hope for is a version of what Rawls has called 'reflective equilibrium'[1] in which our pieties are brought into relation with our more critical opinions, and modified accordingly, while in their turn influencing our reasoned judgements. Much of the moral question of animals concerns piety however, and in this respect we must give up the hope of a fully reasoned answer to it.

CONFLICTS AND ORDERINGS

The motive of morality is complex. Were we immortal beings, outside nature and freed from its imperatives, the moral law would be sufficient motive. But we are mortal, passionate creatures and morality exists for us only because our sympathies endorse it. We are motivated by fellow-feeling, by love of virtue and hatred of vice, by a sense of helplessness and dependence which finds relief in piety, and by a host of socially-engendered feelings which have no place in the serene dispensations of a 'Holy Will'. Hence conflicts and dilemmas arise. The attraction of utilitarianism lies in the promise to resolve all these conflicts by construing moral judgement as a kind of economic calculus. But the promise is illusory and the effect of believing it repulsive. So how are moral conflicts resolved? How, in particular, should we respond to the situation in which the moral law points in one direction, and sympathy another, or in which the ethic of virtue clashes with the ethic of piety?

First, let it be said that the moral law, when it speaks, takes precedence. For the moral law can exist on no other terms. Only if a right guarantees its subject-matter does it offer protection to the one who possesses it. Only then do rights perform their role of defining the position from which moral dialogue begins. The essential function of morality, in creating a community founded in negotiation and consent, requires that rights and duties cannot be sacrificed to other interests.

But rights and duties can conflict. The result is a dilemma, and the distinguishing mark of a dilemma is that, while only one of two things can be done, you have a duty to do both. This duty is not cancelled by the dilemma: you merely have an excuse for not fulfilling it.

When the claims of right and duty have been satisfied, in so far as possible, the claims of virtue must be addressed. Even if the moral law neither forbids nor permits an action, there is still the question whether a virtuous person would perform it. For example, even if we established that animals have no rights, and that we have no duties towards them under the moral law, it would not follow that we can treat them as we choose. It may still be the case – and manifestly is the case – that certain ways of treating them are vicious and that there are only some ways of treating them that a good person would contemplate. This, I believe, is a primary source of moral thinking about animals.

Finally, when all requirements of right and virtue have been met, we can respond to the call of sympathy: and here a kind of utilitarian thinking comes into play, as the means to extend our sympathies to all whose interests are affected by our acts. Even so, the authority of this reasoning is not absolute: for sympathy may compete with piety. A common case is mercy killing. Our sympathy for the victim of some terrible disease leads us to wish for the ordeal to be quickly over. Piety forbids that we destroy the human frame. The conflict here is painful partly because the sources of our conflicting emotions are so far apart. We therefore try to rationalise our pieties by measuring them against our sympathies and discipline our sympathies by testing against the intuitions which stem from piety. The dialectic of sympathy and piety provides a second major source of moral thinking about animals.

While this ordering of the four sources of moral reasoning may be questioned, and while it leaves much unresolved, it corresponds, I believe, to the practice of the ordinary conscience and accords with the underlying function of morality, as I envisage it.

7

THE MORAL STATUS OF ANIMALS

NON-MORAL BEINGS

The account of moral reasoning that I have just sketched offers an answer, even if not a fully reasoned answer, to the question of animals. In developing this answer, I shall use the term 'animal' to mean those animals that lack the distinguishing features of the moral being – rationality, self-consciousness, personality, and so on. If there are non-human animals who are rational and self-conscious, then they, like us, are persons, and should be described and treated accordingly. If *all* animals are persons, then there is no longer a problem as to how we should treat them. They would be full members of the moral community, with rights and duties like the rest of us. But it is precisely because there are animals who are not persons that the moral problem exists. And to treat these non-personal animals as persons is not to grant to them a privilege nor to raise their chances of contentment. It is to ignore what they essentially are and so to fall out of relation with them altogether.

The concept of the person belongs to the ongoing dialogue which binds the moral community. Creatures who are by nature incapable of entering into this dialogue have neither rights nor duties nor personality. If animals had rights, then we should require their consent before taking them into captivity, training them, domesticating them or in any way putting them to our uses. But there is no conceivable process whereby this consent could be delivered or withheld. Furthermore, a creature with rights is duty-bound to respect the rights of others. The fox would be duty-bound to respect the right to life of the chicken and whole species would be condemned out of hand as criminal by nature. Any law which compelled persons to respect the rights of non-human species would weigh so heavily on the predators as to drive them to extinction in a short while. Any morality which really attributed rights to animals would therefore constitute a gross and callous abuse of them.

Those considerations are obvious, but by no means trivial. For they point to a deep difficulty in the path of any attempt to treat animals as our equals. By ascribing rights to animals, and so promoting them to full membership of the moral community, we tie them in obligations that they can neither fulfil nor comprehend. Not only is this senseless cruelty in itself; it effectively destroys all possibility of cordial and beneficial relations between us and them. Only by refraining from personalising animals do we behave towards them in ways that they can understand. And even the most sentimental animal lovers know this, and confer 'rights' on their favourites in a manner so selective and arbitrary as to show that they are not really dealing with the ordinary moral concept. When a dog savages a sheep no one believes that the dog, rather than its owner, should be sued for damages. Sei Shonagon, in *The Pillow Book*, tells of a dog breaching some rule of court etiquette and being horribly beaten, as the law requires. The scene is most disturbing to the modern reader. Yet surely, if dogs have rights, punishment is what they must expect when they disregard their duties.

But the point does not concern rights only. It concerns the deep and impassable difference between personal relations, founded on dialogue, criticism and the sense of justice, and animal relations, founded on affections and needs. The moral problem of animals arises because they cannot enter into relations of the first kind, while we are so much bound by those relations that they seem to tie us even to creatures who cannot themselves be bound by them.

Defenders of 'animal liberation' have made much of the fact that animals suffer as we do: they feel pain, hunger, cold and fear and therefore, as Singer puts it, have 'interests' which form, or ought to form, part of the moral equation. While this is true, it is only part of the truth. There is more to morality than the avoidance of suffering: to live by no other standard than this one is to avoid life, to forgo risk and adventure, and to sink into a state of cringing morbidity. Moreover, while our sympathies ought to be – and unavoidably will be – extended to the animals, they should not be indiscriminate. Although animals have no rights, we still have duties and responsibilities towards them, or towards some of them. These will cut across the utilitarian equation, distinguishing the animals who are close to us and who have a claim on our protection from those towards whom our duties fall under the broader rule of charity.

This is important for two reasons. Firstly, we relate to animals in three distinct situations, which define three distinct kinds of responsibility: as pets, as domestic animals reared for human purposes and as wild creatures. Secondly, the situation of animals is radically and often irreversibly changed as soon as human beings take an interest in them. Pets and other domestic animals are usually entirely dependent on human care for their survival and well-being; and wild animals, too, are increasingly dependent on human measures to protect their food supplies and habitats.

Some shadow version of the moral law therefore emerges in our dealings with animals. I cannot blithely count the interests of my dog as on a par with the interests of any other dog, wild or domesticated, even though they have an equal capacity for suffering and an equal need for help. My dog has a special claim

THE MORAL STATUS OF ANIMALS

on me, not wholly dissimilar from the claim of my child. I caused it to be dependent on me precisely by leading it to expect that I would cater for its needs.

The situation is further complicated by the distinction between species. Dogs form life-long attachments and a dog brought up by one person may be incapable of living comfortably with another. A horse may be bought or sold many times, with little or no distress, provided it is properly cared for by each of its owners. Sheep maintained in flocks are every bit as dependent on human care as dogs and horses; but they do not notice it and regard their shepherds and guardians as little more than aspects of the environment, which rise like the sun in the morning and depart like the sun at night.

For these reasons, we must consider our duties towards animals in three separate ways: as pets, as animals reared for our purposes and as creatures of the wild.

PETS

A pet is an honorary member of the moral community, though one relieved of the burden of duty which that status normally requires. Our duties towards these creatures in whom, as Rilke puts it, we have 'raised a soul', resemble the general duties of care upon which households depend. A man who sacrificed his child or a parent for the sake of his pet would be acting wrongly; but so too would a man who sacrificed his pet for the sake of a wild animal

towards which he has had no personal responsibility –
say by feeding it to a lion. As in the human case, moral
judgement depends upon a prior assignment of
responsibilities. I do not release myself from guilt by
showing that my pet starved to death only because I
neglected it in order to take food to hungry strays; for
my pet, unlike those strays, depended completely on
me for its well-being.

In this area, our moral judgements derive not
only from ideas of responsibility but also from our
conception of human virtue. We judge callous people
adversely not merely on account of the suffering that
they cause but also, and especially, for their thought-
lessness. Even if they are calculating for the long-term
good of all sentient creatures, we are critical of them
precisely for the fact that they are calculating, in a
situation where some other creature has a direct claim
on their compassion. The fanatical utilitarian, like
Lenin, who acts always with the long-term goal in
view, loses sight of what is near at hand and what
should most concern him and may be led thereby, like
Lenin, into unimaginable cruelties. Virtuous people
are precisely those whose sympathies keep them alert
and responsive to those who are near to them,
dependent on their support and most nearly affected
by their heartlessness.

If morality were no more than a device for
minimising suffering, it would be enough to maintain
our pets in a state of pampered somnolence, awakening them from time to time with a plate of their

favourite tit-bits. But we have a conception of the fulfilled animal life which reflects, however distantly, our conception of human happiness. Animals must flourish according to their nature: they need exercise, interests and activities to stimulate desire. Our pets depend upon us to provide these things – and not to shirk the risks involved in doing so.

Pets also have other and more artificial needs, arising from their honorary membership of the moral community. They need to ingratiate themselves with humans and therefore to acquire their own equivalent of the social virtues. Hence they must be elaborately trained and disciplined. If this need is neglected, then they will be a constant irritation to the human beings upon whose goodwill they depend. This thought is obvious to anyone who keeps a dog or a horse. But its implications are not always appreciated. For it imposes on us an obligation to deal strictly with our pets, to punish their vices, to constrain their desires and to shape their characters. In so far as punishment is necessary for the education of children, we regard it as justified: parents who spoil their children produce defective moral beings. This is not merely a wrong towards the community; it is a wrong towards the children themselves, who depend for their happiness on the readiness of others to accept them. Pets must likewise be educated to the standards required by the human community in which their life, for better or worse, is to be led.

Furthermore, we must remember the ways in

which pets enhance the virtues and vices of their owners. By drooling over a captive animal, the misanthrope is able to dispense more easily with those charitable acts and emotions which morality requires. It is in no way surprising that Hitler, for example, sentimentalised animals and lived among pets. The very same man who commanded the murder of six million innocent people and the torture and ruin of millions more, was the first European leader to outlaw hunting, on the grounds that animals are innocent and that to hunt them is cruel. The sentimentalising and 'kitschification' of pets may seem to many to be the epitome of kind-heartedness. In fact it is very often the opposite: a way of enjoying the luxury of warm emotions without the usual cost of feeling them, a way of targeting an innocent victim with simulated love that it lacks the understanding to reject or criticise, and of confirming thereby a habit of heartlessness. To this observation I shall return.

Pets are part of a complex human practice, and it is important also to consider the nature of this practice and its contribution to the well-being of the participants. Even if we fulfil all our obligations to the animals whom we have made dependent, and even if we show no vicious motives in doing so, the question remains whether the net result of this is positive or negative for the humans and the animals concerned. There are those who believe that the effect on the animals is so negative, that they ought to be 'liberated' from human control. This dubious policy exposes the animals to risks for which they are ill-prepared; it also shows a remarkable indifference to the *human* suffering that ensues. People depend upon their pets, and for many people a pet may be their only object of affection. Pets may suffer from their domestication, as do dogs pent up in a city flat. Nevertheless, the morality of the practice could be assessed only when the balance of joy and suffering is properly drawn up. In this respect the utilitarians are right: we have no way of estimating the value of a practice or an institution except through its contribution to the total good of those involved. If it could be shown that, in the stressful conditions of modern life, human beings could as well face the prospect of loneliness without pets as with them, then it would be easier to condemn a practice which, as it stands, seems to make an indisputable contribution to the sum of human happiness, without adding sensibly to that of animal pain.

We should also take note of the fact that most pets exist only because they are pets. The alternative, for them, is not another and freer kind of existence, but no existence at all. No utilitarian could really condemn the practice of keeping pets therefore, unless he believed that the animals in question suffer so much that their lives are not worthwhile.

This point touches on many of our modern concerns. We recognise the increasing dependence of animals on human decisions. Like it or not, we must accept that a great many of the animals with which we are in daily contact are there only because of a human choice. In such circumstances, we should not hasten to criticise practices which renew the supply of animals while at the same time imposing upon us clear duties to look after them.

ANIMALS FOR HUMAN USE AND EXPLOITATION

The most urgent moral questions concern not pets but animals which are used for specific purposes – including those which are reared for food. There are five principal classes of such animals:

- beasts of burden, notably horses, used to ride or drive
- animals used in sporting events – for example, in horse-racing, dog-racing, bull-fighting and so on
- animals kept in zoos or as specimens
- animals reared for animal products: milk, furs, skins, meat and so on
- animals used in research and experimentation.

No person can be used in any of those five ways; but it does not follow that an animal who is so used will suffer. To shut a horse in a stable is not the same act as to imprison a free agent. It would normally be regarded as conclusive justification for shutting up the horse, that it is better off in the stable than elsewhere, regardless of its own views in the matter. Such a justification is relevant in the human case only if the victim has either forfeited freedom through crime or lost it through insanity.

The first two uses of animals often involve training them to perform activities that are not natural to them but which exploit their natural powers. Two questions need to be addressed. First, does the training involve an unacceptable measure of suffering? Second, does the activity allow for a fulfilled animal life? These questions are empirical and cannot be answered without detailed knowledge of what goes on. However, there is little doubt in the mind of anyone who has worked with horses, for example, that they are willing to learn, require only light punishment and are, when properly trained, the objects of such care and affection as to provide them with ample reward. It should be added that we have one reliable criterion of enjoyment, which is the excitement and eagerness with which an animal approaches its work. By this criterion there is no doubt that greyhounds enjoy racing, that horses enjoy hunting, team-chasing and cross-country events in which they can run with the herd and release their energies, and even that terriers enjoy, however strange this seems to us, those dangerous adventures underground in search of rats and foxes.

But this should not blind us to the fact that sporting animals are exposed to real and unnatural dangers. Many people are exercised by this fact, and particularly by the conduct of sports like horse-racing and polo, in which animals are faced with hazards from which they would normally shy away and which may lead to painful and often fatal accidents. Ought we to place animals in such predicaments?

To answer such a question we should first compare the case of human danger. Many of our occupations involve unnatural danger and extreme risk – soldiering being the obvious example. People willingly accept the risk in return for the excitement, status or material reward which attends it. This is a normal calculation that we make on our own behalf and also on behalf of our children when choosing a career. In making this calculation we are motivated not only by utilitarian considerations but also by a conception of virtue. There are qualities which we admire in others and would wish for in ourselves and our children. Courage, self-discipline and practical wisdom are promoted by careers in which risk is paramount; and this is a strong reason for choosing those careers.

Now animals do not freely choose a career, since long-term choices lie beyond their mental repertoire. Nevertheless, a career may be chosen *for* them; and, since the well-being of a domesticated animal depends upon the attitude of those who care for it, its career must be one in which humans have an interest and which leads them to take proper responsibility for its health and exercise. The ensuing calculation may be no different from the calculation undertaken in connection with a human career. The risks attached to horse-racing, for example, are offset, in many people's minds, by the excitement, abundant feed and exercise and constant occupation which are the horse's daily reward, and by the human admiration and affection which a bold and willing horse may win.

But this brings us to an interesting point. Because animals cannot deliberate and take no responsibility for themselves and others, human beings find no moral obstacle to breeding them with their future use in mind. Almost all the domestic species that surround us have been shaped by human decisions, bred over many generations to perform by instinct a task which for us is part of a conscious plan. This is especially true of dogs, cats and horses, and true for a different reason of the animals which we rear for food. Many people feel that it would be morally objectionable to treat humans in this way. There is something deeply disturbing in the thought that a human being should be bred for a certain purpose or that genetic engineering might be practised on the human foetus in order to secure some desired social result. The picture painted by Aldous Huxley in *Brave New World* has haunted his readers ever since, with a vision of human society engineered for happiness and yet deeply repugnant to every human ideal. It is not that the planned person, once grown to maturity, is any less free than the normal human accident. Nevertheless, we cannot accept the kind of manipulation that produced him, precisely because it seems to disrespect his nature as a moral being and to assume a control over his destiny to which we have no right. This feeling is an offshoot of piety and has no real ground either in sympathy or in the moral law.

Pious feelings also forbid the more presumptuous kind of genetic engineering in the case of animals. There is a deep-down horror of the artificially created monster which, should it ever be lost, would be lost to our peril. Yet the conscious breeding of dogs, for instance, seems to most eyes wholly innocent. Indeed, it is a way of incorporating dogs more fully into human plans and projects, and so expressing and enhancing our love for them. And there are breeds of dog which have been designed precisely for risky enterprises, like the terrier, the husky and the St Bernard, just as there are horses bred for racing. Such creatures, deprived of their intended career, are in a certain measure unfulfilled, and we may find ourselves bound, if we can, to give them a crack at it. Given our position, after several millennia in which animals have been bred for our purposes, we have no choice but to accept that many breeds of animal have needs which our own ancestors planted in them.

Once we have understood the complex inter-action between sporting animals and the human race, it seems clear that the same moral considerations apply here as in the case of pets. Provided the utilitarian balance is (in normal circumstances) in the animal's favour, and provided the responsibilities of owners and trainers are properly fulfilled, there can be no objection to the use of animals in competitive sports. Moreover, we must again consider the human values that have grown around this use of animals. In Britain, for example, the horse race is an immensely important social occasion: a spectacle which does not merely generate great excitement and provide a cathartic climax, but which is a focus of elaborate social practices and feelings. For many people a day at the races is a high point of life, a day when they exist as eager and affectionate members of an inclusive society. And animals are an indispensable part of the fun – imparting to the human congress some of the uncomplicated excitement and prowess upon which the spectators, long severed from their own instinctive emotions, draw for their heightened sense of life.

Indeed, history has brought people and animals together in activities which are occasions of individual pleasure and social renewal. Take away horse-racing, and you remove a cornerstone of ordinary human happiness. This fact must surely provide ample justification for the risks involved. It does not follow that horse-racing can be conducted anyhow, and there are serious questions to be raised about the racing of very young horses who, when so abused, are unlikely to enjoy a full adult life thereafter. But, provided the victims of accidents are humanely treated, such sports cannot be dismissed as immoral. Indeed, we have a duty to encourage them as occasions of cheerful association between strangers.

INFLICTING PAIN

The same could be said, it will be argued, about practices which are morally far more questionable, and which have in some cases been banned by law in Britain: dog and cock fighting, for example, and bear-baiting. For many people the Spanish bullfight comes into this category. For in these cases pain and injury do not arise by accident, but are deliberately inflicted, either directly or by animals which are set upon their victim and encouraged to wound and kill. We must distinguish three cases:

- the deliberate infliction of pain for its own sake and in order to enjoy the spectacle of suffering
- the deliberate infliction of pain in order to achieve some other purpose, to which pain is a necessary means
- the deliberate embarking on an action of which pain is an inevitable but unwanted by-product.

The first of those is morally wrong – and not because it turns the balance of suffering in a negative direction. It would be wrong regardless of the quantity of pleasure produced and regardless of the brevity of the suffering. It is wrong because it displays and encourages a vicious character. Spectacles of this kind contribute to the moral corruption of those who attend them. Sympathy, virtue and piety must all condemn such activities, and the fact that they are the occasions of enjoyment and social life cannot cancel the corruption of mind from which the enjoyment springs.

As the argument of the last chapter implies, the utilitarian calculus applies only when it is also the voice of sympathy; wicked pleasures are not better but worse than wicked pains. If dog-fights must occur, it is a better world in which they are observed with pain than one in which they are observed with pleasure.

Given that dog-fights and bear-baiting involve the deliberate infliction of suffering for its own sake and with a view to enjoying the result, they must surely be condemned. But not every deliberately inflicted pain is to be compared with these cases. Animals cannot be trained without the occasional punishment, and punishment must be painful if it is to have the desired effect. The punishment is inflicted, however, not for the sake of the pain, but for the sake of the result. If this result could be achieved without pain, then it would be right to choose the painless path to it. If it is far better for a horse or a dog to be trained than otherwise, then it is no cruelty but kindness to inflict whatever pain is necessary to secure this end.

The infliction of fear is governed by a similar principle. Many of our dealings with animals involve the deliberate infliction of fear – as when a flock of sheep is shepherded by dogs. But again, it is not the fear that interests the shepherd, but the control of his flock, which can be effectively moved by no other means.

Here we come up against a teasing question, however. Just how much pain, and how much fear, are we entitled to inflict, in order to secure our purposes? In answering such a question it is necessary to distinguish the case where the good aimed at is a good for the animal itself, and the case where the animal is sacrificed for the good of others. This distinction is fundamental when dealing with human beings, who can sometimes be hurt for their own good, but rarely hurt for the good of another. But it seems to apply to animals too.

Many animals suffer at our hands, not in order to improve their own condition, but in order to provide pleasure to others: for example, when they are killed in order to be eaten. How much pain, and of what kind, can then be tolerated? Most people would say, the minimum necessary. But what is necessary? Animals destined for the table can be killed almost painlessly and with little fear. But religious beliefs may rule this out. Ritual slaughter in the Muslim tradition requires a death that is far from instantaneous, in circumstances calculated to engender terror. Yet the pain and fear are still, in one sense, necessary – necessary, that is, to ritual slaughter. Some people might therefore conclude that ritual slaughter is immoral. But that does not alter the fact that it can be carried out by decent people, who neither welcome nor enjoy the pain and who believe that there is no legitimate alternative, short of vegetarianism.

Or take another example: the bullfight, that last

surviving descendant of the Roman amphitheatre, in which so many innocent animals, human and non-human, were once horribly butchered. There is no doubt that all I have said in praise of horse-racing as a social celebration applies equally to bullfighting. Nevertheless, in a bullfight great pain is inflicted, and inflicted deliberately, precisely because it is necessary to the sport: without it, the bull would be reluctant to fight and would in any case not present the formidable enemy that the sport requires. The spectators need take no pleasure in the bull's sufferings; their interest, we assume, is in the courage and skill of the matador. Nevertheless, many people feel that it is immoral to goad an animal in this way, and to expose other animals, like the horses of the picadors, to the dire results of its rage.

Even in this case, however, we must see the animal's sufferings in context. Only if the spectators' interest were cruel or sadistic could it be condemned out of hand; and the question must arise whether bulls have a better time, on the whole, in a society where they end their lives in the arena than in societies where there is no use for them except as veal. Let it be said that Spain is one of the few countries in Europe where a male calf has a life-expectancy of more than a year. At the same time, it is hard to accept a practice in which the courage of the matador counts for everything and the sufferings of his victim are so thoroughly disregarded. Surely, it might be said, this displays a deficit of the sympathy which we ought to bestow on all creatures whose sufferings we have the power to alleviate?[1]

The third case of inflicting pain – in which suffering is the unwanted by-product of a deliberate action – will concern me when I come to consider our relations to animals in the wild. Before moving on I shall consider the remaining cases of animals who are reared and kept for human purposes.

ZOOS

Some animals are happier in zoos than others. Big cats, wolves and similar predators enter a deep depression when confined and it is only to be regretted that the sight is not more distressing to the average visitor than it seems to be. It cannot be said of zoos, as I have said of horse-racing, that the suffering of the animals is offset by any vital social benefit. True, there are benefits of other kinds. You can learn much from zoos and from time to time a species can be saved from extinction by its captive members – though the general reluctance of animals to breed in these circumstances can only be a further sign of how unsuited they are to live in them.

The only plausible answer to the problem of zoos is to argue that they should be so organised as to cause minimum distress to their inmates who, while deprived of many of their natural joys, can at least be assured of a kindly death and a life of comfortable somnolence. The morality of keeping wild animals in these conditions is nevertheless questionable, given that so little of human life depends on it. Some animals, like monkeys and donkeys, become tame in zoos and cease to struggle against their confinement. But what is the point of a zoo if its inmates are tame? And is there not something ignoble in the desire to see a wild animal in conditions of total safety, when the poor creature, raging against the gaping crowd of spectators, cannot punish their insolence with its teeth and claws? The least that can be said is that zoos make no contribution to the store of human virtue.[2]

LIVESTOCK AND THE EATING OF MEAT

It is impossible to consider the question of farm animals without discussing an issue which for many people is of pressing concern: whether we should consume animal products in general and meat in particular. To what sphere of moral debate does this question belong? Not, surely, to the moral law, which offers no decisive answer to the question of whether it is wrong to eat a *person*, provided he or she is already dead. Nor to the sphere of sympathy, which gives few unambiguous signals as to how we should treat the dead remains of living creatures. Our only obvious guide in this area is piety which, because it is shaped by tradition, provides no final court of appeal. In the Judaeo-Hellenic tradition, animals were sacrificed to the deity and it was considered an act of piety to share a meal prepared for such a distinguished guest. In the Hindu tradition, by contrast, animal life is sacred and the eating of meat is as impious as the eating of people.

In the face of this clash of civilisations there is little that the sceptical conscience can affirm, apart from the need for choice and toleration. At the same time, I cannot believe that a lover of animals would be favourably impressed by their fate in Hindu society, where they are so often neglected, ill-fed and riddled with disease. Having opted for the Western approach, I find myself driven by my love of animals to favour eating them. Most of the animals which graze in our fields are there because we eat them. Sheep and beef cattle are, in the conditions which prevail in English pastures, well-fed, comfortable and protected, cared for when disease afflicts them and, after a quiet life among their natural companions, despatched in ways which human beings, if they are rational, must surely envy. There is nothing immoral in this. On the contrary, it is one of the most vivid triumphs of comfort over suffering in the entire animal world. It seems to me, therefore, that it is not just permissible, but positively right, to eat these animals whose comforts depend upon our doing so.

I am more inclined to think in this way when I consider the fate of human beings under the rule of modern medicine. In comparison with the average farm animal, a human being has a terrible end. Kept alive too long by processes like the organ transplant, which nature never intended, we can look forward to years of suffering and alienation, the only reward for which is death – a death which, as a rule, comes too late for anyone else to regret it. Well did the Greeks say that those whom the gods love die young. It is not only divine love but also human love that expires as the human frame declines. Increasingly, many human beings end their lives unloved, unwanted and in pain. This, the greatest achievement of modern science, should remind us of the price that is due for our impieties. How, in the face of this, can we believe that the fate of the well-cared for cow or sheep is a cruel one?

Two questions trouble the ordinary conscience, however. First, under what conditions should farm animals be raised? Secondly, at what age ought they to be killed? Both questions are inevitably bound up with economics, since the animals in question would not exist at all if they could not be sold profitably as food. If it is uneconomical to rear chickens for the table, except in battery farms, should they therefore not be reared at all? The answer to such a question requires us to examine the balance of comfort over discomfort available to a chicken, cooped up in those artificial conditions. But it is not settled by utilitarian considerations alone. There is the further and deeper question, prompted by both piety and natural sympathy, as to whether it is right to keep animals, however little they may suffer, in conditions so unnatural and so destructive of the appetite for life. Most people find the sight of pigs or chickens, reared under artificial light in tiny cages, in conditions more appropriate to vegetables than to animals, deeply disturbing and this feeling ought surely to be respected, as stemming from the primary sources of moral emotion.

Those who decide this question merely by utilitarian calculation have no real understanding of what it means. Sympathy and piety are indispensable motives in the moral being and their voices cannot be silenced by a mere calculation. Someone who was indifferent to the sight of pigs confined in batteries, who did not feel some instinctive need to pull down these walls and barriers and let in light and air, would have lost sight of what it is to be a living animal. His sense of the value of his own life would be to that extent impoverished by his indifference to the sight of life reduced to a stream of sensations. It seems to me, therefore, that a true morality of animal welfare ought to begin from the premise that this way of treating animals is wrong, even if legally permissible. Most people in Britain agree with that verdict, although most do not feel so strongly that they will pay the extra price for a free-range chicken or for free-range eggs. To some extent, of course, people are the victims of well-organised deception. By describing chickens and eggs as 'farm fresh', producers effectively hide the living death upon which their profits depend. But customers who are easily deceived lack one important part of human virtue. Travellers in the former communist countries of Eastern Europe, for example, would do well to ask themselves why meat is so readily available in shops and restaurants, even though no animals whatsoever are visible in the fields. A Czech *samizdat* cartoon from the communist years shows two old women staring sadly into a vast factory farm, full of cows. One of them remarks to her companion: 'I remember the days when cows had souls'; to which her companion replies 'yes, and so did we'. The cartoon was intended as a comment on communism; but it points to the deep connection that exists between our way of treating animals and our way of treating ourselves.

Suppose we agree that farm animals should be given a measure of their natural freedom. The question remains as to when they should be killed. To feed an animal beyond the point at which it has ceased to grow is to increase the cost to the consumer, and therefore to jeopardise the practice to which its life is owed. There is no easy solution to this problem, even if, when it comes to calves, whose mournful liquid eyes have the capacity to raise a cloud of well-meaning sentiment, the solution may seem deceptively simple. Calves are an unavoidable by-product of the milk industry. Male calves are useless to the industry and represent, in existing conditions, an unsustainable cost if they are not sold for slaughter. If we decide that it really is wrong to kill them so young, then we must also accept that the price of milk – on which human children depend for much of their nourishment – is at present far too low. We must, in other words, be prepared to accept considerable human hardship, in particular among poorer people, in order to satisfy this moral demand. It is therefore very important to know whether the demand is well-grounded.

Young animals have been slaughtered without compunction from the beginning of history. The lamb, the sucking pig, the calf and the leveret have been esteemed as delicacies and eaten in preference to their parents, who are tough, coarse and over-ripe by comparison. Only if there is some other use for an animal than food is it economical to keep it past maturity. Mutton makes sense as food only in countries where wool is a commodity. Elsewhere sheep are either kept for breeding or eaten as lambs. Beef cattle, too, await an early death, as do porkers. We could go on feeding these animals beyond the usual date for slaughter but this would so increase the price of meat as to threaten the habit of producing it and therefore the lives of the animals themselves.

In the face of this, we surely cannot regard the practice of slaughtering young animals as intrinsically immoral. Properly cared for, the life of a calf or lamb is a positive addition to the sum of joy, and there can be no objection in principle to a humane and early death, provided the life is a full and active one. It is right to give herbivores the opportunity to roam out of doors on grass, in the herds and flocks which are their natural society; it is right to allow pigs to rootle and rummage in the open air, and chickens to peck and squawk in the farmyard, before meeting their end. But when that end should be is more a question of economics than of morals.

In short, once it is accepted that animals may be eaten, that many of them exist only *because* they are eaten, and that there are ways of giving them a fulfilled life and an easy death on their way to the table, I cannot see that we can find fault with the farmer who adopts these ways when producing animals for food. Those who criticise farmers may often have reason on their side; but there is also a danger of self-righteousness in criticisms offered from a comfortable armchair by people who do not have the trouble of looking after farm animals and see only their soft and endearing side. Farmers are human beings and no less given to sympathy than the rest of us. And a good farmer, rearing sheep and cattle on pasture, keeping dogs, cats and horses as domestic animals, and free-range chickens for eggs, contributes more to the sum of animal welfare than a thousand suburban dreamers, stirred into emotion by a documentary on television. Such people may easily imagine that all animals are as easy to deal with as the cat which purrs on their knees, and whose food comes prepared in tins, offering no hint of the other animals whose death was required to manufacture it. It would be lamentable if the moral highground in the debate over livestock were conceded to those who have neither the capacity nor the desire to look after the animals whose fate they bewail, and not to the farmers who do their best to ensure that these animals exist in the first place.

EXPERIMENTS ON ANIMALS

There is no humane person who believes that we are free to use animals as we will just because the goal is knowledge. But there are many who argue that experiments on live animals are nevertheless both necessary for the advance of science (and of medical science in particular), and also permissible when suitably controlled.

It seems to me that we must consider this question in the same spirit as we have considered that of livestock. We should study the entire practice of experimentation on live animals, the function it performs and the good that it produces. We should consider the fate of the animals who are the subject of experiment and the special duty of care that might be owed to them. Finally, we should lay down principles concerning what cannot be done, however beneficial the consequences – and here our reasoning must derive from sympathy, piety and the concept of virtue, and cannot be reduced to utilitarian principles alone.

Medical research requires live experimentation and the subjects cannot be human, except in the cases where their consent can reasonably be offered and sought. It is not only humans who benefit from medical research: all animals within our care have an interest in it, and the assumption must be that it is so conducted that the long-term benefits to all of us, human and animal, outweigh the short-term costs in pain and discomfort.

The duty of care owed to animals used in medical

research is to ensure that their lives are worth living and their suffering minimised. Even within these constraints, however, there are certain things that a decent person will not do, since they offend too heavily against sympathy or piety. The sight of the higher mammals, subject to operations that destroy or interfere with their capacities to move, perceive or understand, is so distressing that a certain measure of callousness is required if these operations are to be conducted. And that which can be done only by a callous person, ought not to be done. The case is comparable to the battery farm. But it is also crucially different. For an experiment is typically conducted on a healthy animal, which is *singled out* for this misfortune and the life of which may be deliberately destroyed in the process. The relentless course of science will always ensure that these experiments occur. But that is part of what is wrong with the relentless course of science.

And here we touch on a question so deep that I doubt that ordinary moral thinking can supply the answer to it. As I hinted above, the advance of medical science is by no means an unmixed blessing. The emerging society of joyless geriatrics is not one at which the human spirit spontaneously rejoices. And although discoveries cannot be undiscovered, nor knowledge deliberately undone, there is truth in the saying that ignorance – or at least ignorance of a certain kind – is bliss. Piety once set obstacles in the path of knowledge – and these obstacles had a function; for they prevented the present generation from seizing control of the earth's resources, and bending them to the cause of its own longevity. Medical science may have benefited the living; but it threatens the resources which the dead laid by for us, and on which the unborn depend. Animals were once sacrificed to the gods by people who cheerfully accepted that they would soon follow their victims to oblivion. Now they are sacrificed to science by people who nurture the impious hope that they can prolong their tenancy forever. This may be morally acceptable. But something in the human heart rebels against it.

WILD ANIMALS

We have no duty of care towards any specific wild animal – to assume otherwise is to deny that it is wild. Duties towards animals are assumed but not imposed. Hence there is a real moral difference between the person who allows his terrier to kill wild rats and the person who keeps tame rats for his terrier to kill. We are surely right in thinking that the second practice is more vicious than the first, even if it causes no more suffering. For it involves the daily violation of an assumed duty of care.

On the other hand, wild animals are part of the environment, and our general (and growing) responsibility towards the environment extends to them. And it is surely right that we take their joys and sufferings into account – not to do so is to fail in sympathy and to assume the kind of arrogant relation towards the natural order which sorts ill with our new found consciousness of our responsibilities towards it. However, this introduces a great complication into our dealings with wild animals. For here our concern is not, primarily, for the individual, but for the species. The individual enters our concern only contingently, so to speak, as when a rabbit steps into the headlights of the car that we are driving. Although we recognise a general duty to take account of the individual's interests in such circumstances, our primary moral concern in daily life must be for the fate of species and for the balance of nature on which they depend. Too much concern for the individual may in fact harm the species, by promoting its diseased or degenerate members, or by preventing necessary measures of population control – something that has been witnessed in the case of the Australian kangaroo.

Here we should recognise a permanent source of moral confusion in the favouritism that we extend to certain species on account of their appearance, their charm, or their nearness to the species that we have adopted as pets. Beautiful animals like the deer, the fox and the badger take precedence over animals like the rat which instinctively repel us, regardless of their intelligence, relative destructiveness or ability to accommodate the needs of humans. We are deeply concerned about the fate of the elephant and the tiger but largely indifferent to that of the toad and the stick insect, despite the equal ecological difficulties under which these four species now labour.

Moreover, some wild animals are more useful to us than others. Some can be eaten, others can provide clothing, ornaments, oils and medicines. Others are destructive of our interests – killing chickens, rifling larders, undermining houses or even threatening life and limb. We cannot maintain the same attitude to all of them – unless it be some serene Hindu passivism which, in modern circumstances, when the balance of nature depends upon human efforts to preserve it, can hardly be promoted as in the best interests of the animals themselves.

Finally, even if we put sentimentality and self-interest aside, we must still recognise relevant differences between the species. To the extent that our moral duties arise from sympathy, we must inevitably respond selectively – not to do so would be a mark of hardness. Some species can, in the right circumstances, befriend us: the elephant, for example, and the dog. Others, even if they have no affection for humans, deal gently and affectionately with their own kind, as mammals must do with their offspring. Others still, while seemingly devoid of affection, are nevertheless curious towards and interested in the world in ways which excite our concern. And, as I remarked above, there is a great difference between those to which we are able to relate as individuals and those which, because they cannot learn from their experience, will always be for us no more than examples of their kind.

Thus it is only with a certain strain that we can care for the well-being of individual insects, even though we recognise that they suffer pain and fear, and are often hungry and in need like the other animals. And fish too lie beyond the reach of natural sympathy: being aquatic, cold-blooded and slimy to the touch, they exist behind an impassable screen of strangeness. Moreover, we have a great interest in keeping fish at such a distance. For not only are they extremely useful as food; there is a sport in catching them which, while painful and frightening to the fish, is a source of one of the greatest and most popular of human relaxations.

In the light of all that, how can we form a coherent moral attitude to animals in the wild? In the absence of any specific duty of care, we must act, I believe, on the following principles:

- we must maintain, so far as possible, the balance of nature
- we are entitled to intervene in the natural order to defend our own interests (after all, we too are part of nature)
- in matters such as hunting, culling and so on, the interests of all the animals involved should be considered, including the humans
- our dealings with wild animals should be measured against the demands of sympathy, piety and human virtue; hence it will be as wrong to take pleasure in the suffering of a wild animal as in the suffering of

a domestic animal, to use wild animals in vicious ways and so on.

Each of those principles seems to follow from preceding arguments. But it is worth considering their application to two controversial instances: angling and fox-hunting. Obviously, a purely philosophical argument will not settle once and for all the complex moral questions that these activities have prompted – the facts are in dispute and feelings run too high. But that does not alter the fact that it is precisely in these controversial areas that a serious moral argument should be put to the test.

Angling

There are many ways of catching fish, but angling differs from most of them in that it is primarily a sport and not a way of getting food. It is also of great environmental significance, since it provides human beings with a pressing interest in maintaining unpolluted waterways and in preventing the destruction of river banks and their flora. It offers a positive contribution to the balance of nature and also to the well-being of the hunted species – conceived, that is, as a species, and not as a collection of existing individuals. By the first of our principles it is unquestionable that angling is morally permissible.

The second principle also applies. It is surely permitted to intervene to preserve the stocks of huntable fish, even though this means destroying predators and taking a robust stand against diseases which, in the natural order of things, might have been better left to run their course. It can hardly be regarded as immoral to extract pike from inland waterways – always assuming that the process is carried out with the minimum of suffering. It is true that environmental activists have advocated a return, in these circumstances, to the real balance of nature, meaning the balance that would exist, were humans to play no part in producing it. (Some have even advocated the reintroduction of wolves on these grounds, as the 'correct' way to reduce the highland deer population, at present dependent on the arduous work of the deer-stalker.) Such proposals are surely unrealistic: for humans would still be taking the initiative in maintaining the balance, and predators would still be instruments of an environmental policy initiated and maintained by humans. Humans, too, are part of the balance of nature and the only serious question is whether they maintain that balance or destroy it. Besides, these radical proposals ignore the moral question: the question of how we should treat the animals concerned. Morality involves taking sides; and while nobody could blame the pike for its behaviour (since it lies, as a non-moral being, beyond all blame), our vestigial sympathy for its victims ought surely to rule out any special pleading on its behalf. And it is hard to believe that those who would introduce wolves as a means of controlling the deer population have much sympathy for deer. Whether hunted by hounds or stalked by humans, a stag is killed at last with a clean shot from a gun; when chased by wolves it suffers the worst of available deaths: the death inflicted on an animal by creatures smaller than itself.

The third principle applies in very much the way that it applied to horse-racing. Angling is an abundant source of human happiness – to many people the image of peace and the preferred way of passing their leisure hours. It is also a social institution through which friendships are formed and cemented, neighbours united and the competitive instinct peacefully exercised. From any utilitarian standpoint, it makes a massive contribution to the sum of human happiness, a fact abundantly displayed in our art and literature. If we are to consider the interests of all the animals involved, then we must surely place this fact in the balance, along with the equally evident fact that the angler's quarry is maintained and protected by those who hunt it. The downside is great: for fish caught on a line suffer both pain and fear, as is evident from their behaviour.[3] At the same time, however great the suffering, we should recognise that it is, in an important sense, necessary. Of course, you could kill fish instantly with a gun or a stick of dynamite. But this would be 'unsporting': that is to say, it would give to the fish no chance, and to the angler a cheap advantage which destroys his sport.

This indicates an important aspect of our fourth principle when applied to such activities as angling.

Traditional forms of hunting often generate and depend upon an ethic of combat, which arises spontaneously in the contest with the quarry. The roots of this ethic lie partly in our piety towards the works of nature. But there is an anticipation too of the human morality of warfare. The hunter tends to have a special respect for his quarry and a desire to offer a fair chance in the contest between them. There are certain things which he feels are owing to the quarry and of which it would be unfair to deprive him. Not that the animals appreciate this chivalrous behaviour. But it is a part of human virtue – a kind of shadow version of justice – to display it, and only a vicious hunter would use every means in his power to trap or kill his prey. Although angling causes more suffering to the fish than an electric current or a stick of dynamite, therefore, we rightly condemn these latter ways of fishing as barbarous.

Our fourth principle is therefore satisfied by angling, at least in its gentler versions. The suffering involved is necessary in that it could be avoided only by destroying the sport. And although there may be sadistic people who take pleasure in the pain of the fish and others who are so unconcerned by its sufferings as to make no efforts to minimise them, these people are not entering into the true spirit of the sport. Serious anglers respect their quarry, are gentle when they can be (for example, when extracting the hook) and regard the sport as an equal contest governed by the rules of fair play. It seems to me that there is nothing vicious in this and therefore no grounds for a moral condemnation.

Fox-hunting

The fox is a predator and a potential nuisance, whose charming appearance does nothing to cancel its notorious habits. Foxes are therefore pursued for two reasons – as pests and as sport. There is tension between these motives, since people wish to get rid of pests but not to get rid of the animals that they hunt for sport. Hence pests have a greater chance of surviving where they are also hunted. On the other hand, it is precisely the sport of fox-hunting that is criticised on moral grounds. When a keeper shoots the fox that has been terrorising his birds, his action seems to arouse little indignation in the public conscience; but when the same fox is pursued by hounds, themselves followed by a crowd on horseback, the strongest protests may be made. It does not seem to me, in the light of the four principles enunciated above, that these protests are really justified.

Foxes thrive in copses, hedgerows and on the edges of pastures, where they can enjoy both cover and open stretches in which to run down or cut off their prey. To preserve this habitat is to favour many species besides the fox – rabbits, hares, voles, field-mice, badgers and a host of lesser animals in which people have little or no sporting interest. It is self-evident, in these circumstances, that fox-hunting makes a positive contribution to the balance of nature. Hunting with hounds has made its own very special contribution to the landscape, providing a motive to conserve the coverts, woods, hedgerows and pastures which have fallen victim to mechanised farming in almost every place where hunting with hounds has disappeared. It is also species-specific: properly trained hounds go after no quarry other than the one that they are trained to pursue and furthermore, if they catch it, kill it instantly. Our first principle therefore finds no fault with fox-hunting and the second principle will apply as readily as in the case of angling.

The third principle would also seem to favour the sport. Anyone who doubts that hunting with hounds has been a rich source of human social life and happiness need only consult our literary and artistic tradition, in which this pursuit is celebrated perhaps above all others, as the picture of human joy. From Homer to Trollope, hunting scenes provide the high points of intensity in the description of human leisure, while both painters and composers have devoted some of their greatest efforts to portraying or evoking the hunt. The judgement of art is confirmed by those who take part in the sport and if it were a case of considering human interests alone, there would be no doubt which way the utilitarian calculus would point.

Moreover, unlike angling, hunting with hounds generates intense pleasure for animals – for the hounds themselves and for the horses which excitedly follow them and who are raised to heights of eagerness which quite transcend the daily hedonic diet of their species. Much of the pleasure felt by those who ride to hounds derives from sympathy with horse and hound – a grateful sense of being returned to the realm of innocent joy in which these favourite creatures are moving.

Against this great accumulation of human and animal delight, it would be difficult to count the fear and pain of the fox as an absolute moral obstacle, unless they were shown to be either so great as to outweigh any amount of pleasure, or unnecessary, or the object of some vicious attitude. The questions here are complex and not surprisingly hunting with hounds remains, and perhaps will always remain, controversial – as it already was when Plato, in *The Laws*, wrote in support of it as the highest form of hunting.

It is, or ought to be, widely recognised that the death of the hunted fox is, when it occurs, more rapid than its death when shot (unless shot in favourable circumstances by an expert marksman), or its death from any rival method commonly employed to despatch it.[4] Moreover, it is certain. If it is pain that concerns us, then I doubt that we will think it great enough to rule against the sport. It is certainly no greater, and probably less, than the pain of the rat caught by a terrier, or the mouse caught by a cat. It is rather the fox's fear, and the relentless pursuit which enhances it, which raise the most serious moral concerns. If the fox does not run and surrenders to an early and instant death, there can be no sport. Hence he must run and only fear will compel him.

Many people dislike this, not because the fear in question outweighs the pleasure of those in pursuit, but because there is something callous in pursuing a creature so relentlessly. In other words, it is the fourth of our principles that is held to apply and which motivates those who most seriously object to hunting. It seems to them that the pleasure involved is either vicious in itself or an expression of a vicious nature. Here, therefore, is where any defence of hunting would have to begin: by showing that the human interest in this sport is compatible with sympathy and virtue.

As in the case of angling, however, we must be careful to distinguish legitimate from illegitimate pleasures. Roy Hattersley, writing in the *Guardian*, made the following remark:

> 'I have long supported whoever it was who said that the real objection to fox-hunting is the pleasure that the hunters get out of it . . . If killing foxes is necessary for the safety and survival of other species, I – and several million others – will vote for it to continue. But the slaughter ought not to be fun.'[5]

The suffering of the caught fish is not fun, but only the price of fun. To describe it as fun is to imply that the angler takes pleasure in the suffering of his quarry, and this is manifestly not true. If there were a sport exactly like angling except that the fish were lifted from the water and then tortured with hooks to the amused shrieks of the bystanders, we should regard it in quite another moral light from the sport of angling. Likewise, if there were a sport which consisted of capturing and then torturing a fox, where the goal of the sport was precisely to inflict this suffering, we should all agree with Mr Hattersley's peremptory judgement. But fox-hunting is not like that. Sometimes, no doubt, such sports are abused by sadists; and it might be right for Parliament to examine the matter, so as to ensure that the rules laid down by the Anglers' Association and the Masters of Fox-Hounds Association not only forbid such abuse, but also have the force of law. But the purpose of such a law would be not to forbid the pleasure of those whom Mr Hattersley describes as 'the hunters' (meaning, no doubt, the followers), but to forbid pleasure of the wrong kind. Otherwise all pleasures bought at the cost of animal suffering must be forbidden – from the eating of meat, through horse-racing and dog-racing, to angling, shooting and hunting with hounds.

Nor should we neglect the extraordinary role assumed by hunting in the rural community, as farmers open their land to their neighbours, and justify their ownership of the land by briefly renouncing their claim on it. This too is a form of piety and, like every pious urge, stems from our sense that we are stewards and tenants, not absolute owners, of the world in which we live. It is this attitude, more than any other, that we must foster, if our species is to survive. And if ever we should lose it, our survival would not be justified in any case.

The counter-argument should not be dismissed, however, and the case remains open. Its interest lies in showing that the deep moral questions will never be answered by our first three principles alone. Environmental, pragmatic and utilitarian arguments all count in favour of fox-hunting. But the real question of its morality is a question of human vice and virtue. And this is invariably the case in our dealings with wild animals. What really matters is the attitude with which we approach their joys and sufferings. When Jorrocks praised hunting as 'the image of war with only five and twenty per cent of the danger' he was consciously praising the human virtue which it displays and encourages. And no reader of Surtees can doubt that, whatever vices are displayed in the hunting field, sadism towards the fox is rarely one of them.

If, on the other hand, it is always wrong to take pleasure in an activity which exposes an animal to the risk of suffering and death, then the condemnation of fox-hunting must extend by parity of reasoning to all field sports – to shooting, stalking and angling. Few people who attack fox-hunting seem prepared to go this far. This is surely a sign that they do not, after all, regard the element of pleasure as in itself an insuperable objection. Indeed, the more one examines the antagonism that fox-hunting arouses, the more elusive do its foundations seem. For this reason I have added an appendix to this book, which explores some of the feelings invoked in the human heart by hunting – feelings towards which modern people, for understandable reasons, are profoundly ambivalent.

8

DUTY AND THE BEAST: MORAL CONCLUSIONS

A SUMMARY OF PRINCIPLES

My argument has ranged freely over abstract metaphysics, ethical philosophy and moral casuistry. In the arguments of Singer and his followers I find much casuistry, little ethical philosophy and no serious metaphysics. This explains the exhortatory simplicity of their conclusions. But it also suggests, to my way of thinking, the extent to which serious questions have been begged. So here, for the benefit of the sceptical reader, is a summary of the principles which I believe ought to guide us in our dealings with animals, and which reflect not only the social function of moral judgement, but also the mental reality of the animals themselves.

- We must distinguish moral from non-moral beings. The first exist within a web of reciprocal rights and obligations created by their dialogue. The second exist outside that web and it is both senseless and cruel to try to bind them into it.

- Animals therefore have no rights. But this does not mean that we have no duties towards them. Duties to animals arise when they are assumed by people, and they are assumed whenever an animal is deliberately made dependent on human beings for its individual survival and well-being.

- Even when no such duty of care has been assumed, our dealings with animals are governed by moral considerations. These considerations derive not from the moral law but from the other three roots of moral feeling: virtue, sympathy and piety.

- The ethic of virtue condemns those ways of dealing with animals which stem from a vicious motive. For example, delight in the suffering of animals is morally abhorrent. So, I take it, is the sexual use and abuse of animals.

- The writ of sympathy may run where the ethic of virtue is silent. For sympathy extends to all creatures with intentionality – all creatures with a view on the world and whose pains and pleasures can be understood as we understand our own.

- When sympathy speaks, its voice has a utilitarian accent. By this I mean that sympathy – true sympathy, that is – takes account of all the creatures involved, even if it does not accord an equal weight to their interests. But utilitarian considerations cannot override rights and duties: they arise only after the demands of the moral law have been met.

- Towards creatures without intentionality – such as

insects and worms – we experience only a shadow form of sympathy. It shows no defect in people that they should take account only of the species, and not of the individual, when dealing with creatures of this kind.

- Our moral obligations towards animals whom we have caused to depend upon us are distinct from our obligations towards animals in the wild. Towards the first we have a duty to provide a fulfilled life, an easy death and the training required by their participation in the human world. Towards the second, we have a duty to protect their habitats, to secure, as best we can, the balance of nature, and to inflict no pain or fear that is not a necessary part of our legitimate dealings with them. Exactly which dealings *are* legitimate is a complicated question. But the above principles go some way towards settling it. To take an animal into captivity for no reason other than to display it in a zoo is morally dubious. To torment an animal purely for the pleasure of doing so is immoral. But the hunting and shooting of wild animals may, in the right circumstances, be permissible and even a positive good.

- The difficult cases arise when we assume a duty of care towards animals who are not granted honorary membership of the moral community. The two most urgent cases are those of farm animals, and especially animals reared for food, and laboratory animals, especially those subjected to painful experiments. In the first case, it seems to me, the demands of morality are answered when animals are given sufficient freedom, nourishment and distraction to enable them to fulfil their lives, regardless of when they are killed, provided they are killed humanely. In the second case, the demands of morality are met only with difficulty, and only on the assumption that the experiments in question make an unmistakable contribution to the welfare of other creatures.

I do not claim that those principles are the last word in the matter. On the contrary, they seem to me only a first word. Rightly understood, however, they should encourage us to distinguish virtuous from vicious conduct towards other species and help us to see why it is that virtuous people may engage in activities like raising pigs for slaughter, eating meat, fishing with a line, wearing furs, or shooting crows and rabbits, which many observers of the human world have denounced as depraved.

SENTIMENTALITY
This leads us, however, to a vice which certainly does infect our dealings with the animal kingdom – the vice of sentimentality. Many of the questions I have discussed have been so clouded by sentimentality that it is worth offering an account of it, in order to show how it arises and how we should respond when we feel its pressure.

Sentimental feeling is easy to confuse with the real thing – for, on the surface at least, they have the same object. The sentimental love of Jane and the real love of Jane are both directed towards Jane, guided by the thought of her as lovable. But this superficial similarity marks a deep difference. A sentimental emotion is a form of self-conscious play-acting. For the sentimentalist it is not the object but the subject of the emotion which is important. Real love focuses on another individual: it is gladdened by his pleasure and grieved by his pain. The unreal love of the sentimentalist reaches no further than the self and gives precedence to pleasures and pains of its own, or else invents for itself a gratifying image of the pleasures and pains of its object. It may seem to grieve at the other's sorrow but it does not really grieve. For secretly, sentimentalists welcome the sorrow which prompts their tears. It is another excuse for the noble gesture, another occasion to contemplate the image of a great-hearted self.

It is clear why animals provide an occasion for sentimental emotions. For animals cannot answer back. They cannot puncture our illusions. They allow us complete freedom to invent their feelings for them, to project into their innocent eyes a fantasy world in which we are the heroes, and to lay our phoney passions before them without fear of a moral rebuke. It is also clear why sentimentality is a vice. It consumes our finite emotional energies in self-regarding ways and numbs us to realities. It atrophies our sympathies by guiding them into worn and easy channels, and so destroys not only our ability to feel but also our ability to help where help is needed and to take risks on behalf of higher things.

As I have argued in this book, sympathy for animals is a natural and noble emotion. But the real sympathy for animals, like the real sympathy for people, has a cost attached to it. Real sympathy obliges us to know animals for what they are, to regard their bad points as well as their good and to take an undeceived approach to their needs and sufferings.

When it comes to wild animals, an unsentimental love embraces what is wild and free in their nature. It respects their habitats, takes an active interest in their way of life, refrains from taming them or from creating any greater dependence on our benevolence than is necessary for a mutual accommodation. It looks on wild animals realistically, neither denying what is unpleasant in their natures nor exaggerating what is beautiful. This love of wild animals is natural to those who live in the countryside and is shared by the majority of those who hunt or shoot them, paradoxical though this may seem. Unfortunately, however, the countryside is now patrolled by day-trippers, whose vision of animal life has been acquired from sentimental story books and sanitised nature programmes on television. It is such people who feel most strongly that activities like hunting, ferreting and hare-coursing, for example, are morally wrong.

Sentimentalists turn a blind eye to unpleasant

facts and their feelings skate rapidly over the rabbits, pheasants and chickens who must die at the fox's behest. Besides, if they were in charge, the fox would be gently dissuaded from its habits, in return for a bowl of canned meat, delivered each morning by some official manager of the countryside, wearing the uniform of the RSPCA.

As for the bowl of canned meat, it will be produced quite painlessly, like the bloodless joint which our sentimentalist takes from a shelf in the supermarket, the history of which has never really been a concern. Anybody who was really disturbed by animal suffering would be far more troubled by the practice of poisoning rats than by that of hunting foxes. But rats do not look right. A fox's mask resembles the face of an alert and interesting human; the face of a rat is sneaky and full of intrigue, while its colour, legs and tail belong to a subterranean world which to us is the world of the tomb. The fox therefore provides a suitable object for those pretend emotions through which sentimentalists fortify their image of themselves as heroes of compassion.

Because they belong to the workings of fantasy, sentimental emotions respond far less easily to reason than do real feelings. Sentimentality involves too large a dose of self-deception to allow the critical intelligence into its precinct. It is for this reason that the arguments I have given about angling will strike a chord in most people, while those, of equal force, about hunting will make little impact on those who are most vigorously opposed to the sport. This would matter less were it not for the natural tendency of sentimentality, in its more angry forms, to lean towards self-righteousness and to forbid that of which it disapproves. Those who hunt, shoot or fish have a real interest in protecting their quarry and in maintaining the ecological balance that ensures its survival. If sentimentality were to prevail, however, this ecological balance might easily be destroyed by ill-considered legislation. The countryside could be turned into a zoo, organised on Disneyland principles and policed by para-military volunteers from the suburbs, prepared to prosecute anybody who should damage a badger sett, pursue a fox or shoot a pigeon.

We should remember that it is not only individual animals which are of concern to us; we have a duty of care towards the environment, without which no animal life would be possible. And sentimental dealings with animals, precisely because they bypass the complexities which are now inevitable in our dealings with the natural world, are by no means favourable to our precarious ecology. When mink farms were first introduced to Britain in the twenties and thirties, a previous generation of sentimentalists, outraged by the idea that animals should be raised for their furs, released them into the wild. The resulting ecological catastrophe has still not been overcome: for mink are voracious consumers of the eggs and young of other species. Waterways have been denuded of many of their traditional inhabitants and birds which were once abundant in our countryside are now on the lists of protected species. Moreover, there is no easy way to control the mink, which is too small, lithe and amphibious to be an easy target. Only with the development of the mink hound, trained to track the animal in its natural habitat, has a comparatively humane way been discovered of reducing the nuisance. But mink-hounds are difficult to train and confined to a few localities. Moreover, they stand to be outlawed, along with all other hunting hounds. This would leave us with no environmentally acceptable weapon against the mink save trapping, which, because it subjects an animal to hours of helpless terror, must surely be the most cruel means of pest control.

I give that example not only because it has again become topical, but also because it shows the natural tendency of sentimental emotion to rush to short-term conclusions over issues where only long-term policies could conceivably do justice to the many conflicting interests. But it will be rightly objected that morality does not suffice for human government and that it is the business of law, not morality, to take the long-term view. The conscience is never clear when abstracted from the here and now, and even if we are rightly suspicious of sentimental feeling, we should be wrong to dismiss the short-term view itself, when morality has no other view on anything.

THE MORAL BEING AND CITIZENSHIP

The moral being is also a political animal – a *zoon politikon*, in Aristotle's famous words. In other words, moral beings live in communities which are organised neither by instinct nor by the ever-flowing emotion of the herd, but by laws and procedures which are consciously chosen and consciously enforced. Their collective life exists on many planes. They are private individuals, bound by affection to family and friends. They are gregarious adventurers, making agreements with others, entering partnerships and joining clubs and institutions. And they are citizens who assume the benefits and responsibilities of political life. A citizen bears a special relation to other citizens – a relation of responsibility and mutual support which binds strangers as well as neighbours, enemies as well as friends. No animal could understand this relationship, still less play a part in sustaining it.

One of the remarkable results of the movement for 'animal rights', however, has been the extension of a kind of shadow citizenship to animals. For many British people, animals resident on British soil enjoy a special relationship to the crown and ought not to be transported to France, where conditions are very different and outside 'our' control. If we compare our vast expenditure of energy and resources on behalf of 'British' animals with our comparative indifference to the animals of Egypt or Uzbekistan, we shall be struck by a singular fact: that it is neither the ease with which our own animals can be helped nor their comparative need which determines our concern for them, but our sense of them as fellow citizens. The RSPCA, which possesses £100 million of accumulated funds, could spend this money in Egypt and produce enormous relief to animals which are suffering in ways that are unthinkable in Britain; while here at home, the Society must actively search for the cases of cruelty which will justify its charitable status. It is true that the RSPCA has made commendable efforts to alert people to the fate of animals in other countries and to offer relief where this is practical. But its donors are not deeply interested and would certainly give far less and with far less conviction if the Society were to divert its resources from the animals 'at home'. There is no question of the RSPCA shutting up shop in Britain and moving abroad, any more than there is a question of the National Health Service transferring its operations to the slums of Cairo. Here we have a striking proof of the way in which animals in modern democracies have become part not only of domestic life, but of the web of public concern. Of course, animals are not and cannot be citizens. Even if given the vote they could not use it and while they can be protected by the law, they can neither obey nor defy it.

The moral question of how animals should be treated spills over, therefore, into a political question of how they should be treated by the law. As we shall see, these questions are by no means the same, and a rational answer to one of them may not dictate a rational answer to the other.

MORALITY AND THE LAW

9

I have given what I believe to be a true account of our moral duties to animals. But the last argument has raised the vexed question of how, if at all, a moral vision should be transcribed into law. It is pertinent to make a few brief remarks in response to this question, by way of a conclusion.

The issues discussed in this work are controversial. Good people with healthy consciences will surely disagree over such questions as to whether hunting, shooting or battery farming are morally reprehensible. It is a long-standing principle of Western constitutional government that, whenever there is substantial moral disagreement, the law should not take sides. Many people disapprove of ritual slaughter, on account of the suffering involved – and they may, in Britain, constitute a majority. But it does not follow that this practice, so central to the religious life of the Jewish and Muslim minorities, should be banned. Others strongly disapprove of the habit of keeping dogs pent up in city dwellings. But by what right could we outlaw a practice on which so many people depend for their peace of mind?

More pertinent still is the case of abortion. Many people think, for good reasons, that abortion is a sin, far greater than any cruelty perpetrated on a dumb animal. A substantial minority, however, regards abortion as morally permissible and also believes that a woman's right to happiness weighs more heavily in the scale of choice than an unborn child's right to life. Hence many who disapprove of abortion concede that Parliament should not outlaw the practice that disturbs them. They recognise that toleration is the price of social harmony, since we must live at peace with people of whose practices we may strongly disapprove.

Even where there is substantial moral agreement, we may feel reluctant to enshrine our moral judgement in law, for fear that to do so would involve too great an encroachment on the liberties of the subject. An example of this is adultery, almost universally disapproved of but not, in our country, forbidden by law. To make this sin, to which so many are tempted, into a crime would be to bind human beings in intolerable chains and so bring the law into disrepute. Still more is it dangerous to legislate on moral grounds against activities like horse-racing or shooting, in which a substantial minority participate and in which they find a joy and fulfilment which they do not regard as immoral at all.[1]

This does not mean that we should never legislate. It means that we should be as clear as possible concerning the ground on which we do so. And the principal ground relates, I believe, to the concept of virtue. I shall illustrate this point with a parallel example.

In our society, all kinds of sexual practices are permitted between consenting adults, provided that they take place in private. However, the publishing of certain kinds of pornographic material, even material in which normal practices are displayed, is forbidden by law. Why is this? Surely because we believe that the *interest* in pornography is corrupt. It is an interest in sex divorced from the moral context provided by human love, an interest which de-personalises the sexual act, makes the object of desire into an object *tout court* and turns sex into a commodity. This interest is wrong not because it does harm to others but because it does harm to the self. The law does not, as a rule, forbid our private actions, provided that they are mediated by consent. But it has an interest in moral corruption, since law is the guardian of society and would be ineffective in a world where the sources of social feeling had all been polluted.

Some ways of treating animals can be compared to pornography in that they minister to a comparable corruption. Dog-fights and bear-baiting, in which the object of interest is (or at any rate, seems to be) the pain, fear and helplessness of an innocent victim, can interest only a hardened heart, and one obsessed by the flesh, by the machinery of suffering, and by the pornography of pain. Like sexual pornography, these practices encourage an interest in the flesh as something objective, curious and without any moral claim on us. They place a veil between the world and our response to it and poison the soul of those who watch them. Such spectacles are naturally forbidden by law, since they threaten the personality of those who attend them.

That is only one example. But it helps us to see why a civilised system of law may permit many immoralities, but nevertheless forbid deliberate cruelty. It can permit ritual slaughter, shooting and horse-racing, in which actual suffering is the known effect of what is done, while forbidding dog-fighting or bear-baiting, in which this suffering becomes an object of interest for its own sake.

There is much more to be said. One thing is clear, however, which is that modern societies suffer from too much legislation concerning matters in which lawyers and politicians are not necessarily the highest authorities. We are faced with a question that humanity is perhaps confronting for the first time in its true form – namely, how to behave towards other species in a world where all of us are competing for survival. The least that can be said is that we should discuss and digest the moral question, before embarking on a legislative solution to it.

APPENDIX 1: THOUGHTS ON FARMING

The outbreak of mad cow disease and the ensuing public panic provide an interesting illustration of the principles advanced in this book. It seems to me that dietary laws of the kind advanced by many religions are, in the first instance, forms of piety. The Jewish law which forbids us to seethe a young animal in its mother's milk may have little sense when considered from the standpoint of a hard-nosed utilitarianism. But our disposition to hesitate before the mystery of nature, to renounce our presumption of mastery, and to respect the process by which life is made, must surely prompt us to sympathise with such an interdiction. And these very same feelings, had we allowed them to prevail, would have caused us to hesitate before feeding to cows, which live and thrive on pasture, the dead remains of their own and other species. It lies in the nature of piety that we can never know the costs of disobeying it: for pious feelings are a confession of ignorance. But the example is a sure proof of the reasonableness of these feelings which lie beyond the reach of reason.

The case illustrates, too, the vaporous nature of human sentimentality. From those who habitually complain against the eating of veal and the tragic destiny of calves dragged from their mothers' teats to the slaughter, we have heard no protest when it is announced that whole herds of animals, young and old, must be marked down for destruction, regardless of whether they are infected with the disease. Yet these are animals towards which we have assumed a duty of care, which have been tended by farmers who are grieved by the thought of killing them for no reason and which have a claim on human protection far beyond the claims of any creature in the wild. We should compare their case with that of the badger, which is, largely on account of its endearing appearance, a 'protected species', and as such an ecological danger of a far greater order than the cow, however treated. Infected with TB, able to roam where it pleases and protected from the only species that could, in modern conditions, control it, the badger is already causing havoc in the countryside and, in all probability, passing its disease to both wild and domestic animals. For the time being, farmers plead in vain for the right to curtail its predations; yet one human case of TB, in some new and frightening strain which can be traced to the badger, would cancel its privileges at once.

Such examples may lead us to wonder whether

anybody really does believe that animals have rights and whether those who make the most noise on behalf of this doctrine might not also be the first to abandon it when the time comes to 'take rights seriously'. They also lead us to consider the extraordinary attitude of the urban consumer to the rural producer, and to recognise the extent to which natural and humane attitudes to domestic animals are being made impossible precisely by those who protest most loudly against the 'cruelty' involved in rearing them.

Animals raised for meat are, for the most part, gregarious, gentle and dependent. They are unhappy in isolation, and emotionally dependent on the proximity of their kind. In the winter they must be sheltered; in the summer, if they are lucky, they are out to grass, or (in the case of the pig and the chicken) free to roam in a place where they can hunt for scraps of food. Human standards of hygiene are alien to their nature, and their affections, unlike ours, are general and transferable, without tragic overtones. Such animals, tended in the traditional way, by a farmer who houses them together in the winter, and allows them to roam in the summer, are as happy as their nature allows. Assuming that their needs are satisfied, only two questions arise in the farmer's mind: when and how they should be killed – for that they must be killed is evident, this being the reason why they live. As I argued earlier, however, death is not merely a moral question. There is an economic aspect which no farmer – and no consumer – can afford to ignore.

Human beings are conscious of their lives as their own; they have ambitions, hopes and aspirations; they are fatally attached to others, who cannot be replaced in their affections but whose presence they feel as a need. Hence there is a real distinction, for a human being, between timely and untimely death. To be 'cut short' before one's time is a waste – even a tragedy. We lament the death of children and young people not merely because we lament the death of anyone, but because we believe that human beings are fulfilled by their achievements and not merely by their comforts.

No such thoughts apply to domestic cattle. To be killed at one year is not intrinsically more tragic than to be killed at two or three. And if the meat is at its best after one year, and if every month thereafter represents an economic loss, who will blame the farmer for choosing so early a death? In so doing he merely reflects the choice of the consumer, upon whose desires the whole trade in meat, and therefore the very existence of his animals, depends.

But what about the manner of death? That it should be quick is not in dispute. Nevertheless, there is a distinction between sudden death and anticipated death, death preceded by terror, and to the conscientious farmer, who has looked after animals from day to day, living with them and providing for their needs, this terror is not merely unwelcome but a betrayal of trust and a dagger of accusation. Livestock farmers therefore prefer to see their animals dispatched suddenly and humanely in the place where they have lived, by skilled slaughterers who know how to kill an animal without awakening it from its soporific routine. Failing that, they will look for a nearby abattoir, where the animals can be taken without the discomfort of a long journey, and without being handed over to some nameless and unanswerable death machine.

EU regulations, interpreted with fanatical zeal by the bureaucrats of MAFF, are destroying these old and humane practices. In a ludicrous rerun of the BSE crisis, unknown and unknowable risks are being put forward as reasons for closing local abattoirs and for forbidding the roving slaughterer. Animals are driven for many miles, to be herded into the death machine by people who have never cared for them, who have no regard for their sufferings, and who see them as no more than living meat on its way to the supermarket.

This is the kind of thing at which humane people should protest. But, as with the BSE crisis, the mere suggestion that there might be a risk to themselves is enough to silence their feeble consciences, to cancel those flutters of grief over doe-eyed calves and panicking porkers, and to whitewash all negative emotions as the bloodless and cellophaned product is taken down from the shelf. What is at risk here, however, is not the consumer – who was never really in jeopardy from the traditional livestock farmer – but the relation between the farmer and his animals. A crucial episode in the care of the herd has been taken from the farmer's hands. Domestic animals have been moved one step further down the ladder from companions to things.

And this, surely, is the moral crux. Livestock farming is not merely an industry – it is a relation, in which man and animal are bound together to their mutual profit, and in which a human duty of care is nourished by an animal's mute recognition of dependency. This alone explains why people will continue in this time-consuming, exhausting and ill-paid occupation, resisting the attempts by bureaucrats and agribusinesses to drive them to extinction. Anybody who cares for animals ought to see this kind of husbandry as a complex moral good, to be defended on the one hand against those who would forbid the eating of meat altogether, and on the other hand against those carnivores who prefer the unseen suffering of the battery farm and the factory abattoir to the merest suggestion of a personal risk.

The life of the cattle farmer is not an easy life, nor is the relation between man and animal as harmonious as it might appear on *The Archers*. Nevertheless, as with all forms of husbandry, cattle farming should be seen in its full context – and that means, as a feature of the total ecology of the countryside. Traditional livestock farming involves the maintenance of pastureland, properly enclosed with walls or hedges. Wildlife habitats spring up as the near-automatic by-products of the boundaries and shady places required by cattle. And in winter there will be unoccupied fields of grass which lend themselves to hunting. Hence many cattle farmers ensure that coverts exist for the support of foxes. In turn the hunt will collect dead stock from the fields, either to feed it to the hounds or to dispose of it without charge. The symbiotic relation between the livestock farmer and the hunt has shaped the English landscape, ensuring that it retains its dual character as producer of human food and complex wildlife habitat, with a beauty that is inextricably connected to its multifarious life. In this way, what is, from the point of view of agribusiness, an extremely wasteful use of land, becomes, from the point of view of the rest of us – both human and animal – the kindest use of land that men have yet devised.

With that observation, however, we enter controversial territory. For many people, hunting with hounds is, or ought to be, a crime.

APPENDIX 2: THOUGHTS ON HUNTING

Nature and culture used to be seen as contrasting elements in our human constitution. But nature is now a product of culture. Not only does human society shape the environment; it is human choice that marks off what is 'natural', and which elevates the distinction between the natural and the artificial to its sovereign place in the moral order. The natural world now depends on our efforts to conserve it and therefore on our judgement as to what belongs to it. Moreover, our very perception of this world as 'natural' is an artefact, formed and nurtured by religion, literature, art and the modern media. When we seek our consolation in nature we are looking in a mirror that we created for this purpose. Nature smiles back at us with human features, since we have carefully ensured that it has no other. All that is truly threatening, alien and mysterious has been cut from the picture: what remains is a work of art. We strive to preserve it from that other and artificial world –

the world of machinery, spoliation, production, consumption and waste. But both worlds are our creation and we can fight only for the boundary between them, hoping that the part which consoles us does not dwindle to the point where consolation becomes a memory.

Nature, as we have invented it, is a source of the beautiful; but it has ceased to be a source of the sublime. For we meet the sublime only when we are confronted with our own littleness and are troubled by forces that we cannot control. The experience of the sublime vanished at the moment when Burke and Kant defined it: their descriptions were a kind of valediction, inspired by the premonition of a world entirely subject to human mismanagement.

None of that alters the fact that the contrast between the natural and the artificial is an immovable part of our worldview and one of the cultural values to which we cling. We need this contrast because we need to see our actions in terms of it. We need to distinguish those impulses which belong to mother nature from those which involve bids for freedom. And we need to relate to other creatures for whom there is no such contrast: creatures whose behaviour stems from nature alone. It matters to us that we should be in constant relation to animals – and wild animals especially. For we seek an image of innocence, of the world before our own depredations, the world *without* man, into which man comes as an intruder. The burden of self-consciousness is lightened by this image: it shows us that we walk on firm ground, where the burden may from time to time be set down and upon which we may rest from our guilt. All this is beautifully captured in the opening pages of Genesis and the vision of Paradise – absurd though it may be from the Darwinian perspective – is the perfect symbol of the natural world as it would be, had we been able to produce it unaided, and without relying on the raw material of evolution.

The desire for a natural order is perhaps unknown to those who are truly part of it. But it is an immovable given in the lives of all civilised beings and, even if it cannot be satisfied, it will exert its power over our thinking and make itself known both in the life of the mind and in the life of the body. It burst upon us in the writings of Rousseau, and his egregiously sentimental vision of the state of nature has exerted its charm over many subsequent writers. But it appeared in a more moderate and intriguing form in the writings of the German romantics, three of whom – Schelling, Hegel and Hölderlin – helped to forge the picture of our condition which has since proved most persuasive and to which I pay tribute in what follows.

According to this picture, human history shares the structure of human consciousness; the individual life is a microcosm of the species, which is in turn, for Hegel, a microcosm of the universal *Geist*. The human soul and human society are both founded in a condition of innocence or 'immediacy', in which they are at one with the world and with themselves. And each grows away from this one-ness through a process of sundering and alienation, as it comes to recognise the otherness by which it is surrounded and upon which it depends. Finally each attains its redemption, as it is restored to the wholeness from which it began, but at a higher plane – the plane of understanding. Just as the individual self is realised by transcending its self-alienation and becoming fully and completely known to itself, so is society fulfilled when the primitive unity with others is rediscovered, but in the form of a self-conscious and law-guided order.

Wherever we look in the modern world, we find this image of our condition actively colonising people's plans and projects. Almost everything that is believed in, almost everything for which a real sacrifice is made, has the character of a *Heimkehr* – a return from alienation, destruction and despair, to an image of home. But not home in its innocence. Rather home transfigured, become conscious of itself, and emancipated from the taint of bondage.

It is this image which dominates the thinking of the environmental movements of our time and also of the campaigners for animal rights who are so often in conflict with them. Both are haunted by the idea of a primitive unity between man and nature, in which other species have an equal weight to our own. Both are appalled by the accelerating presumption which has alienated man from nature and set him at odds with the order upon which he nevertheless depends. And both look forward to a restored unity with the natural world – a unity achieved not by innocence but by understanding, and by the self-knowledge and self-discipline which come from accepting our limitations.

Myths are necessary to human life and are part of the price we pay for consciousness. Moreover, even if they give a distorted view of history, they frequently give insight into the human psyche. Planted in us, too deep for memory, and beneath the layers of civilisation, are the instincts of the hunter-gatherer, who differs from his civilised descendants not only in making no distinction between the natural and the artificial order, but also in relating to his own and other species in a herd-like way. The hunter-gatherer is acutely aware of the distinction between men and women; he quickly unites with his fellows in a common enterprise and is focused by nothing so much as the chase. He is a spontaneously cooperative being, who cooperates not only with his own species but also with those that are most readily adapted to join in his hunting: with horse, hound, falcon and ferret. Towards his prey he takes a quasi-religious attitude. The hunted animal is hunted as an individual – and the instinct to hunt in this way has an obvious ecological function. (Buffalo Bill was the very antithesis of the hunter-gatherer, a degenerate by-product of the civilising process.) But the hunted species is elevated to divine status as the totem and a kind of mystical union between the tribe and its totem seals the pact between them. The experience of the hunter involves a union of opposites – absolute antagonism between individuals resolved through a mystical identity of species. By pursuing the individual and worshipping the species, the hunter guarantees the eternal recurrence of his prey. Totemism is part of the natural ecology of the tribe and its ubiquity is far better explained by its ecological function than by the far-fetched ideas of Freud and Malinowski.[1]

In Ovid's *Metamorphoses* the stories are told of the halcyon, the nightingale, and so on. These creatures embody in their species-being a soul which, in human shape, had been the soul of an individual. The thought is metaphysically incoherent. But it is part of the normal repertoire of the hunter-gatherer to think in some such way. And the idea of the species-soul is still with us. For the fisherman, the individual trout on his line is also The Trout, the universal whose soul he knows in many instances and which he loves with the greater passion in the moment when he pits himself against the mere individual who is its passing instance. This attitude is exalted by totemism into a religious idea: the universal species becomes a sacred object, to which the particular quarry is a sacrifice. The quarry dies on behalf of the species and thereby reconsecrates the sacred identity between species and tribe.

This way of relating to animals is less familiar to

those who know only pets. For domestic animals have a kind of personality bestowed by our daily dealings. We treat them as individuals and they learn to respond as such. The hunter-gatherer, in his original condition, has little room for such an attitude. In time, however, he learns to enhance his powers by cooperating with other species – in particular with hound and horse.

The hunter now works side by side with animals whom he treats as individuals, in hot pursuit of the prey whose individuality is lent to it only temporarily, as it were, and because it has been singled out by the chase. The horse beneath him is Sam or George, whose habits he knows and with whom he communicates directly. The hounds to whom he calls are Saviour, Sanguine and Sawdust; he addresses them by name, aware of their individual virtues and vices, for which he makes constant allowance. But the fox – still known by his totem name as Reynard or Charlie – is the generic being who appears equally in Aesop and Surtees, in La Fontaine and Stravinsky. Charlie is merely incarnate in the hunted animal and will survive its death. For the brief moment of the chase, he is an individual, to be understood through the beliefs and strategies, the vulpine strengths and weaknesses that distinguish this particular instance. Once killed, however, Charlie returns to his archetypal condition, reassuming his nature as The Fox, whom the huntsman knows and loves, and whose eternal recurrence is his deep desire.

Although this return to a previous relation with the natural world is now rare, it helps us to understand some of the longings and frustrations of those who seek it. In the civilised world, where food is not hunted or gathered but produced, hunting and gathering become forms of recreation. But they awaken the old instincts and desires, the old pieties and the old relations with our own and other species. If your purpose in angling is to catch a fish, then how simply this could be achieved with an electrode, which stuns the population of the river bank and brings it unconscious to the surface. But what angler would look on this method with other than disgust? To catch fish in this way is to cross the barrier between the natural and the artificial – it is to conquer another portion of nature for the world of machinery. Yet the point of angling was to return, in however well-protected a guise, to the natural world, the world unblemished by our footsteps. And that is the experience so lyrically evoked by the great tradition of writers, from Isaak Walton to Richard Jefferies, who have celebrated the sport as a therapy for the anxious soul.

More important, however, is the fact that industrial fishing, of the kind deprecated by the angler, is an offence to the totem. It aims indiscriminately at the collective and, instead of sacrificing the individual trout for the sake of the universal Trout, throws the universal itself onto the river bank. Like trawling and drift-netting, it constitutes a threat to the hunted species – and the threat, as we know, is real. (See Appendix 3.) The intentionality of angling is of another kind. It involves a contest between the individual person and the individual animal – a contest which may be lost and which is experienced when successful as a victory and a tribute to the totem.

Why should people wish for this primordial relation with other species and are they justified in pursuing it? To answer these questions it is not enough merely to trace the evolutionary sediment which is stirred by hunting. Nor is it enough to recast the myth from which I began – the myth of man's fall and redemption, and of the homeward journey out of alienation. However suggestive this myth has been to philosophers, artists and writers in the romantic tradition, the fact remains that there is no way back and that the only homecoming that we are offered is the religious one, which promises an *Aufhebung* not here and now but in the unknowable beyond.

As I see the matter, hunting (by which I mean the pursuit of individual animals to the death, as exemplified in angling, ferreting or hunting with hounds) brings into focus the real differences between humans and other animals, and at the same time lifts some of the burden which those differences create. As I have argued in earlier chapters of this book, human beings differ from animals *systematically*. Unlike the other animals with which we come into regular contact, we are self-conscious; our thoughts involve

'I'-thoughts, 'you'-thoughts and 'he, she, we and they'-thoughts. Unlike the animals, we have moral, aesthetic and religious experience; we pray to things visible and invisible; we laugh and grieve; we are indignant, approving and dismayed. And we relate to each other in a special way, through the give and take of practical reason and its associated concepts of justice, duty and right. Human beings are actual or potential members of a moral community, in which each member enjoys sovereignty over his own affairs so long as he accords an equal sovereignty to others. The concepts of right and duty regulate such a community and ensure that disputes are settled in the first instance by negotiation and not by force. And with all this comes an immense burden of guilt. Morality and self-consciousness set us in judgement over ourselves, so that we see our actions and characters constantly from outside, judged by ourselves as we are by others. (It is part of the function of moral dialogue and the concepts of duty, right and justice to generate this external point of view.) We become cut off from our instincts, and even the spontaneous joy of fellowship is diminished by the screen of judgement through which it first must pass.

The hunter-gatherer faces and overcomes the guilt of his condition more easily than we do. The willed identity between the hunter and his tribe, and between the tribe and the universal prey, affirms, for the hunter, his primal innocence. Just as there is no guilt attached to killing when lion kills goat, so are we released from guilt when acting from the imperatives of the species. At the same time, considered as species, the prey is identical with the tribe. Hence this guiltless killing is also a purging of guilt – of the guilt that attaches to the murder of one's kind. The prey becomes a sacrificial victim: the individual who pays with his life for the continuity of the tribe, by attracting the accumulated aggression between the hunters which is the price of their mutual dependence.

Although the conditions no longer obtain, in which totemism could be a real moral force, the desire for guiltless killing endures and attracts to itself a powerful residue of social emotion. Hunting, shooting and fishing are forms of social life. Even when conducted alone – as shooting and fishing might be conducted – they are the focus of clubs, outings, parties, contests and festivals. And those who are familiar with the English countryside will know that hunting is not merely the occasional sport of the wealthy, but an elaborate social artefact, in which all country people from all walks of life participate, and which spills over into horse trials, point-to-points, the pony club, the hunt ball, hunt breakfasts and fun-rides, charity events, puppy shows and farmers' lunches – in short, every available form of social communion. Hunting is also a rehearsal of social instincts and a reaffirmation of our mutual dependence.

It is this, I believe, which explains the extraordinary hold of 'field sports', as they are euphemistically called, over the lives of those who participate in them. There is, in the contest between man and his prey, an inherent social meaning, a summoning into consciousness of the misremembered life of the tribe. Even in angling this is so and, if angling also has its solitary aspect, this is in part because the crucial transition, in which the species becomes incarnate in the individual, can occur only at the end of a single line. It is nevertheless the case that ordinary coarse fishing is a social affair. Much of the joy of angling resides in the concentrated silence of people working side by side along the bank, confident in their neighbours and bound by a common enterprise.

There is another aspect to hunting, however, which also bears on its significance for us, in our attempts to conserve the boundary between the natural and the artificial worlds. Hunting is a territorial activity, and to hunt land and waterways is to exert a claim of ownership. The hunter-gatherer is at no time more attached to his world than when hunting, since hunting is also a 'taking into possession'. (The expression is the one used by the common law, to describe what happens when a wild animal is hunted and killed by the owner of land.) For this reason, hunting rights and game laws have underpinned the structure of ownership and tenancy in our societies, and have been vivid subjects of political dispute. It is hardly necessary to mention the significance of the royal forests, the eighteenth-century game laws, the decree by the French

Revolutionaries that henceforth the people could hunt where they choose, or the monopoly over hunting exerted by the communist Nomenklatura in Eastern Europe. The transcending of the hunter-gatherer economy into the producer economy required that hunting and fishing rights be legally specified and defended. Thereafter you could hunt in a place only if you had the right to do so or were the guest of another whose right it was.

This obvious fact is of some significance. For it has made hunting, shooting and fishing into elaborate forms of hospitality. In all societies, hospitality is a necessary part of ownership, since it is the price paid for the social acceptance of private wealth. Ownership of land is particularly sensitive as it places tangible obstacles in the way of those who do not enjoy it and restricts the supply of every raw material. English law has been lenient and subtle in the distribution of land – granting rights of way and easements, enforcing covenants and prescriptive rights, and producing a unique combination of over-crowding and public access in a landscape which retains its domestic appearance. Nevertheless, even in England, the private ownership of land provokes resentment among those whom it excludes and the Ramblers' Association, for example, has taken an increasingly belligerent line towards farmers who forbid people to cross their property.

The farmer who forbids the rambler is very likely to permit the hunt, regardless of whether he is plagued by foxes and notwithstanding the fact that the hunt does far more damage than a quiet walker in an anorak. The reason is simple. The rambler is an outsider, someone who does not 'belong'. The farmer needs to justify his ownership to his neighbours, to those with whom he lives as one possessor among others. Hospitality extends to them, since they enjoy the same ancestral title to the territory from which his portion has been carved. Hence, when the hunt meets on his land, the farmer will usually offer additional hospitality in order to confirm that the land is open to his guests. In Vale of White Horse country, where I live, it is normal for a farmer to offer port, sausages and cake to followers on horseback and to make special provision for the huntsman, whose partiality to whisky is well-known. Towards ramblers, however, farmers feel no hospitable urges, regarding them as alien intruders who should stick to public rights of way (not of all of which are recognised by the farmers themselves).

Ceremonial hospitality of this kind should be distinguished from ordinary giving. It is an attempt to raise the relations among neighbours to a higher level: to confer legitimacy and permanence on the current patterns of ownership. It is partly in acknowledgement of this that mounted followers wear a uniform and obey a strict dress-code that extends to horse as well as rider. The hunt arrives on the farmer's land not as an ordinary visitor but as a ceremonial presence, endorsing his ownership in the act of exploiting it.

In the hunt, therefore, are revived, in transfigured form, some of the long-buried emotions of
our forebears. The reverence for a species, expressed
through the pursuit of its 'incarnate' instance; the
side-by-sideness of the tribal huntsman; the claim to
territory and the animals who live in it; and the
therapy for guilt involved in guiltless killing.

But is it guiltless? Hunting, shooting and to a
lesser extent angling have been repeatedly condemned as immoral: not immoral *per se*, since they
may well be necessary if people are to feed themselves.
But immoral in circumstances like ours, when
hunting is a recreation rather than a means to food
and clothing. The arguments here are involved and
various, and there is no short answer to them.
Nevertheless, it is not a sufficient justification for
recreational hunting that it puts us in touch with
needed emotions or that it maintains the boundaries
which fence off the 'natural' world. Even if it could be
shown that hunting (in one or other of its many
forms) is the best that we over-civilised beings can
hope for, by way of a homecoming to our natural state
and the best proof against the tribal aggressions which
otherwise beset us, this would carry little weight in
modern times. Many people are also sceptical of the
romantic *Heimkehr*. The best hope for our future,
they believe, is to live with our alienation, to cease to
look for some simulacrum, however sublimated and
self-conscious, of the old tribal emotions and to look
on the world as a vast suburban garden, an artificial

and third-rate paradise, which we must maintain as kindly and responsibly as we can. This means taking the interests of all creatures into account and refraining from pursuits which cause needless suffering, lest the spectacle of suffering should cease to trouble us. The comparative toleration of modern people towards angling stems from the fact that fish are so very different from us, in their appearance, habitat and behaviour, that it is no sign of a hard heart to look on their sufferings unmoved. The hare, the stag and the fox, by contrast, are near to us. Whatever the difference between our thoughts and theirs, we share the circumstances of our pains, our terrors and our death, and to inflict these things on such an animal is to act with a callous disregard.

There is something right in that argument. But it also overlooks the crucial fact from which I began this appendix and which is now at the back of all our minds, including the minds of those opposed to hunting. The natural world can no longer look after itself. We are guardians and keepers of the natural order, which owes its character to us. We could turn our backs on it and cease to interfere. But the result would not be better, either for the animals who live in it or for us, who depend on the natural world for our sense of what we are. If deer were never culled, Exmoor would contain nothing else besides suburban houses, and the highlands of Scotland would be treeless crags. If foxes were never killed, lambs, ducks and chickens would be reared indoors, in conditions that no decent person should tolerate. If angling ceased, our waterways would never be maintained and mink, coote and moorhen would drive all their rivals to extinction. In so far as 'biodiversity' is a wished-for part of our third-rate paradise, culling and pest-control will remain incumbent on us. And it seems to me that the truly callous way of doing these things, is the way that merely attacks the species – as when poisoned bait is laid for rats and foxes, or electric shocks are used to free the waterways of pike. Such practices involve a failure to achieve the 'incarnation' of the species in the individual and so to renew our respect for it. The true graciousness of hunting occurs when the species is controlled through the arduous pursuit of its individual members and so impresses upon us its real and eternal claim to our respect and sympathy. This does not mean that hunting can be pursued in any way we choose. A rifle, in the hands of a well-trained stalker, may be a permissible way to bring death to a stag; but it does not follow that the very same stag might as well be killed by a grenade, a noose or a handgun. An animal like the fox, which can be cleanly killed only in the open and which is never more quickly despatched than by a pack of hounds, requires great labour and the cooperation of three species if he is to be hunted in this way. If he is to be hunted at all, however, this is how it should be done.

The example is controversial and those who believe in the rights of animals will dismiss what I have said as quite irrelevant. On the other hand, I have tried to show in this book that the concept of animal rights is based on a confusion. It is my view that a true understanding of the nature of moral judgement will find no conclusive argument against properly conducted hunting. Indeed, I incline to Plato's view, defended in *The Laws*,[2] that hunting with hounds is the noblest form of hunting. And this because it is the form in which our kindred nature with the animals is most vividly present to our feelings. The pleasure that we feel in this kind of hunting is borrowed from the animals who are really doing it – the hounds who pursue and the horses who follow them. The residual moral doubts are ours, not theirs, and they must be answered by us – by ensuring that the fox or stag has the best chance of saving himself and the quickest death should he be caught.

This appendix is adapted from a longer article, 'From a view to a death: culture, nature and the huntsman's art', which appeared in Environmental Values *(vol. 6, no. 4, 471–82).*

APPENDIX 3: THOUGHTS ON FISHING

Few people feel much tenderness for fish: their bleak, staring eyes and unshifting expressions, their cold blood and slimy skin, their habit of preying on each other, their lack of the mammal's love of offspring – all these combine with the foreign element in which they move to exclude them from our sympathy. Yet fish too feel pain, fish too are sentient, perceiving and thinking creatures, fish too have a life, which may be frustrated or fulfilled, painful or pleasant.[1] What should be our attitude to these creatures, and does the writ of morality run so far as to protect them?

The case is an interesting one for a special reason. The mentality of a fish forbids us from forming any meaningful attachment to it. You can relate to the individual dog or horse or cat, partly because it reciprocates, and partly because its behaviour changes to accommodate your affection. Those fish which seem to respond in a comparable way turn out, on investigation, not to be fish at all, but mammals:

dolphins, walruses, sea-cows, whales or porpoises. *Moby Dick*, perhaps the greatest tale in the literature of hunting, tells of an intense relation between the obsessed Captain Ahab and the White Whale who had crippled him. You can make sense of this story because of the masterly way in which Melville introduces you to the life and sufferings of the whale, eliciting sympathy and even love for these vulnerable creatures, and enabling you to understand that they are not merely a species, but also a collection of individuals, among whom the White Whale, with his burden of knowledge and rage, stands out as the supreme challenge – as much an enemy as the *toro* facing the matador in the bullring, and ten times as intelligent.

To sharks and swordfish, however, we cannot take such an attitude. To consult their interests is to consult, first and foremost, the interests of a species. If we have duties towards them, then it is towards the species. True, we ought not to kill fish cruelly, or to inflict unnecessary pain. But it is hard to think that we could ever acquire the kind of duty of care towards an individual fish that we are constantly acquiring towards domestic animals – and even towards wild mammals and birds, when they seek or find our protection, like the broken-winged eagle in Janáček's *From the House of the Dead*. The loss of a pet goldfish is at once compensated by the provision of another, and to mourn over the individual fish as though nothing could console you, is to show a morbid disregard for the difference between real and phoney relations.

Yet it is precisely when we come to consider our dealings with fish that we discover the extent to which we have discounted their interests. This ought to be of particular concern to the British, who have traditionally been fish-eating people, and yet who seem to have lost all real concern for the future of the oceans from which they once were nourished. Cod – which the Pilgrim Fathers could scoop from the waters of New England in baskets, so abundant was it – has now more or less disappeared from the Atlantic. That which is now served as fish and chips is a caricature of the meal which provided the greatest of our childhood treats; in place of the succulent steaks of full-grown cod, the best we can hope for is the unfrozen relic of a codling, scooped from the bottom of the sea by a floating factory, deprived of life long before it had the chance to give life in its turn, and served up dry, thin and powdery, swamped by the batter which should merely seal in its juices.

The story of cod has been told by Mark Kurlansky[2] and it is a story that is deeply troubling. How could it happen that this wonderful animal, provider of food to generations of human beings, the foundation of our national diet, capable, when properly respected, of replenishing its stocks with an ease that is matched by no other edible species – how is it possible that it should have been brought to the point of extinction? The answer comes pat: 'the tragedy of the commons', 'the prisoner's dilemma', 'the paradox of social choice' – in other words, the process whereby we collectively choose our own undoing, by competing over a dwindling resource with nothing to guide us apart from the 'rational self-interest' which, as all religions warn us, is the enemy of reason.

The Icelanders had a solution: namely unilateral assertion of exclusive rights to the breeding grounds of the cod. In other words, they allowed, or tried to allow, no other players in the game. But this solution, which twice brought Iceland to the verge of war with Britain, is fraught with danger. Moreover, the fish in British waters are no longer ours either to catch or to protect. The Spanish can even demand compensation from us when we try to save the last few mackerel from their nets.

This ought to worry us. It ought to worry the French too. Skate, we now learn, are more or less extinct in the North Sea, where they were recently abundant. And if there is a recipe to match fish and chips for harmony, succulence and the expression of national character, it is surely *raie au beurre noir*. Like cod and chips, this requires thick chunks, taken from large, mature and once happy fish; the tiny wings of murdered babies, which are all that we now see of skate, produce a flat and sodden caricature of the real dish. But skate take twelve years to reach breeding age. Hence there is no chance – *no chance at all* – that they will survive without our protection. And, given

European fishing policy, they will not be protected, since no one has the exclusive right to their breeding grounds.

Fish are disappearing so rapidly that it will soon be too late to save them. Already the local fishmonger – source of cheap food to our parents, and the most cheerful and interesting shop in every high street – has all but disappeared from English towns. Mature fish are rarely found in European waters and appear in the shops only when flown in at vast expense from the Seychelles or the South Atlantic.

International agreements will not solve this problem: for they will be respected only by those like the Icelanders and the British, inheritors of Common Law and the Saxon sense of justice. The only solution so far discovered has been the Icelandic one – the belligerent assertion of a national right to the breeding grounds of an endangered species. But in a world where belligerence is feared, and where animals are invariably its principal victims, this solution too is unavailable. Here then is a problem that is simultaneously moral and political, and for which we seem to have no procedure that will enable us to ensure that the right thing is done.

At the same time we, whose ancestors depended on fish for their survival, owe fish a favour. It is time that we woke up to our very great obligation to these vulnerable and peaceable creatures who have given us so much. They do not touch the hearts of those who campaign for animal rights, and who wax indignant over veal crates or fox-hunts. But their cause is all the more just for that – for it is not a sentimental cause, not a way of showing off one's big-hearted sympathies, of being a cuddly bear among cuddly bears. It is a cause in which human interests and animal welfare coincide, and in which we alone can save the day. It is also a cause which touches our national interest and national identity at the deepest level.

Some see the solution to the problem in the practice of fish-farming. Already there are species which can grow in captivity and furnish food for the table: the salmon, the sea-bass and the prawn being examples. But it has also been persuasively argued that the methods of farming are themselves a threat to the environment, filling the seas with hormone-studded effluent, the effect of which is to poison the breeding grounds of other species. Besides, are we to look with equanimity on a future in which the oceans are entirely dead, apart from those fenced-in sections around our shores, where imprisoned creatures gorge on artificial food, knowing nothing of the wild wide sea which was once their element? Something in human nature rebels against this, just as something in our nature rebels against gratuitous cruelty or the destruction of a great work of art.

In the case of fish, therefore, we confront what is perhaps the most urgent of the moral problems surrounding our relations with animals. We are gradually pushing all other species to a state of dependency, even in those elements, like the air and the sea, which are foreign to us. It is not enough that we can replace the stock of wild fish with our own domesticated varieties: for in doing so we simply hasten the process whereby wild animals, in their natural habitats, are being driven from the world. Only if we believe that the world exists for our convenience, and that no other creatures have a claim on it, can we take this attitude: and it is precisely because that belief is no longer tenable that the moral problems to which this book has been addressed have arisen in their acute modern form.

It seems to me that we should not conclude that it is wrong to eat fish. Fishing for food need not present the fish with any death worse than that to which they are naturally destined and, given the absence of an individual duty of care, the only reason for not fishing is the belief that the stocks could not be replenished, or that the habitat is in some way damaged by our predations. The answer to this is surely to catch fish in such a way that the habitat remains undamaged and unpolluted, with stocks of mature animals constantly replenished.

This means that the extended drift-nets currently employed by European fishermen ought to be condemned; so ought the floating fish-factories, which suck up indiscriminately the life of the oceans, making no distinction between mature and growing fish, and wreaking havoc on the food chain. There is no doubt that, of all the ways of fishing, angling is the most to be commended. Not only is it specific to the individual fish; it also enables the angler to choose whether to return the fish to the water if it is not yet grown, or to keep it if it is mature enough to be eaten without a conscience. The suffering of the individual fish is surely outweighed by the immense benefits conferred on the species – benefits not only in saving it from more extensive human predation, but also in giving people a strong motive to maintain and enhance its habitat.

Sadly angling is a time-consuming activity, and one that could never satisfy the demand for edible fish. The challenge, therefore, is to devise nets that enable fishermen to bring only mature fish on board, and which are species-specific, so that fish whose young would otherwise be trapped by them are either warned off or provided with escape routes. Meanwhile, it seems to me, we have a moral obligation not to eat the young cod, haddock, skate and turbot which are virtually the only examples of these species that appear in our shops. If ever there were a cause for moral protest on behalf of animals, it is this one. For only if we take up this cause will the oceans have another chance to live.

GLOSSARY OF PHILOSOPHICAL TERMS

aesthetic value, aesthetic sense, etc The term 'aesthetic' (from Greek *aesthesis*, sensation or perception) was introduced into philosophy by the German writer AG Baumgarten, and taken up by Kant, who used it to describe the area of human experience associated with natural beauty and the response to works of art. Kant's view is that aesthetic values arise from the inherent need of rational beings not merely to use things but also to contemplate them and to delight in their intrinsic forms. This attitude of contemplation is 'disinterested', and sees things not as means to our purposes but as ends in themselves.

alienation Term often used to translate the German *Entfremdung* (or 'estrangement'), which, in Hegelian philosophy, is the condition in which human consciousness sees itself as object rather than subject, thing rather than person.

anthropomorphism (Greek) The habit of seeing animals, plants and natural phenomena generally as though they had the consciousness and the mental life of people.

appetitive The appetitive aspect of mind is the aspect of desiring, wanting, and striving to get, in which a creature is animated by a goal, and by a conception of the means to achieve it. A raptor in search of prey illustrates this aspect of mental life; a bee looking for pollen probably does not.

asserted/unasserted A sentence may be asserted – as it normally is when uttered in isolation – or unasserted as, for instance, when preceded by the word 'if' or 'then'. 'If John is angry then it would be best to avoid him' contains two sentences, neither of which is asserted by the person who utters the complex that contains them. The ability to think in unasserted sentences is essential to reasoning and to the formulation of hypotheses. If animals cannot entertain unasserted thoughts, then this is one reason for distinguishing their mental life from ours.

Aufhebung Term of Hegelian philosophy, meaning the 'lifting up' of consciousness from one level to a higher level. This occurs when an irreconcilable conflict or contradiction at the first level demands and receives resolution at the second – as the conflict between my perspective and yours is resolved by a bird's-eye view.

beautiful/sublime Following Edmund Burke, Enlightenment (q.v.) thinkers made a distinction among aesthetic values (q.v.) between the beautiful and the sublime, the first arising when we feel at home with the object of aesthetic contemplation, and take pleasure in the harmony between itself and our human nature, the second arising when we are overawed or terrified by it, and yet at the same time moved by its wondrousness and power.

belief A belief is a state of mind which might be true or false, and which can (in the normal instance) be confirmed or refuted by the way things are. Animals have beliefs, to the extent that they can learn from their experience, and modify their behaviour in response to changes in their conception of the world.

Cartesian theory of the mind The theory associated with René Descartes, which holds that the mind is a non-physical entity, known directly only to itself, by introspection, and connected only contingently with the body or behaviour.

categorical imperative The moral law, as stated by Kant, is an imperative, since it tells you what to do, and is categorical, since it is not conditional on what you want. Kant argued that there is one categorical imperative, and that it is the supreme axiom of morality; however, he states it in several ways, of which the most famous is this: 'Act on that maxim which you can will as a law for all mankind (or for all rational beings).' Kant held this to be the proper philosophical basis of the Christian Golden Rule: 'Do as you would be done by.'

cognitive The cognitive aspect of mental life is that concerned with the gathering and assessment of information, and the construction of a mental picture of the world. Its crucial component is belief (q.v.).

charity The disposition to treat others as you would treat yourself, and to extend to them the full benefit of human sympathy.

choice The conscious adoption of a goal, followed by the attempt to achieve it. Animals have desires (q.v.) and are motivated by their desires to do things; but it does not follow that they make choices, since this seems to imply a rational assessment of the goal, and a strategy for achieving it. Philosophers often speak of 'intention' when referring to the faculty of choice, and imply that intention and desire belong to different levels of mental life.

common law The law which forms the basis of the English legal system, and which results not from legislation or the decrees of a sovereign, but from the deliberation of judges, as they strive to find the just solution to specific conflicts and to extract general principles from accepted precedents.

conditioning The connection of a stimulus to a response by repetition. Once thought to be the foundation of learning (q.v.) (e.g. by IP Pavlov); now more often regarded as a degenerate form of it.

consciousness Awareness of the world and of one's own body as a part of it. Many animals have consciousness; but in all probability only human beings have self-consciousness (q.v.).

content The content of a mental state is, roughly speaking, the state of affairs that fulfils or corresponds to it. Thus the content of a belief is the state of affairs that would make it true; the content of a desire is the state of affairs that would satisfy it. Whenever you believe that . . ., desire that . . ., fear that . . ., hope that . . ., the sentence following the word 'that' identifies the content of your state of mind.

cost/benefit Cost-benefit analysis attempts to estimate the case for or against a course of action in terms of the balance of measurable benefits against measurable costs. The use of this analysis outside economics is justifiable only on the assumption that costs and benefits can be quantified. Utilitarianism (q.v.) is based on that assumption.

decision theory A branch of applied mathematics, designed to formalise the notion of rational choice under conditions of risk and uncertainty. An important part of cost-benefit analysis (q.v.), which some have tried to appropriate in order to make sense of moral reasoning.

desire The motive towards something presently lacked, with a view to obtaining it. Many animals have desires, even if they have no rational plans for fulfilling them.

duty One's duty is the act one ought to perform, the non-performance of which is a fault for which one can be, and ought to be blamed.

emotion An emotion is a state of mind which is both a feeling and a motive to action. Fear, for example, is something felt; but we also act out of fear. Emotions typically involve beliefs (q.v.) and desires (q.v.), and like beliefs and desires they may be justified or unjustified.

empirical An empirical statement is one that is based on and justified by experience and investigation, as opposed to an *a priori* or philosophical statement, which is justified (if at all) by abstract reasoning, of the kind given in this book.

Enlightenment The movement of ideas which began

with the scientific revolution in the seventeenth century, and which led to the attempt to give a revised picture of the world and of man's place within it, in which theology (q.v.) would no longer occupy the central place. The 'Enlightenment project' is the concomitant attempt to give foundations for morality, society and political life in purely secular (q.v.) terms, without reference to the commands of God.

erotic love Love for another person based in sexual desire, in which the individual is wanted in and through his body, and yet not wanted merely as a body. A mystery, which philosophers from Plato to Sartre have sought in vain to understand.

ethology The study of behaviour or habit (Greek: *ethos*), specifically the study of animal behaviour, especially in natural conditions.

Geist German: spirit, soul or mind. The general term employed by Hegel and his followers to describe the all-pervasive substance from which mental life, in their view, is composed. The German idealists supposed *Geist* to be the ultimate reality, and the universe to be intelligible as the object of its own self-understanding.

gratitude The disposition to recognise that a good has been freely bestowed upon you, to give thanks to the giver, and to seek to do good in return. A moral emotion, available only to a creature which can understand and act from a conception of the good.

happiness The condition of being consciously contented with what you are and how things are for you. Not the same as pleasure, since it requires a judgement that what you are is also something that it is good to be. Hence, when moralists say that we must aim to maximise happiness, it is not at all clear how we can obey their instructions, while the attempt to define goodness in terms of happiness is very likely to end up in a vicious circle.

Holy Will In Kant's moral philosophy, a will that is free from all contamination of desire, and which passes immediately from the recognition of a duty to its performance.

I-Thou (*Ich-Du*) The form of relation, discussed in quasi-theological terms by the German Jewish philosopher Martin Buber, in which two people relate to each other in the first-person singular, each regarding the other as an irreplaceable self-consciousness, and responding to the other directly and without the mediation of general principles or laws.

imagination The capacity to form a conception of something believed not to be real – as in the creation and understanding of fictions.

indignation Anger at something judged to be wrong: an emotion which lies beyond the repertoire of non-moral animals.

intentionality (Latin: *intendere*, to aim.) A mental state has intentionality if it is directed towards or focused upon an object. For example, fear is fear *of* something, anger is anger *about* or *towards* something etc. Intentionality is a technical term for the mysterious 'aboutness' of our states of mind. No philosopher has yet given a satisfactory account of it, though many have tried.

justice/injustice To treat people justly is to accord to them their rights (q.v.) and their deserts; to treat them unjustly is to violate their rights, to ignore their deserts, or to give them what they do not deserve. The disposition to treat others justly is the virtue of justice. Injustice arises when legitimate claims are knowingly overridden.

learning The process whereby a creature masters the difficulties presented by its environment – by accumulating information, or skills or (in the human case) virtues (q.v.).

logical connectives Terms like 'if', 'and', 'or' etc. which join sentences together and make inference possible – as in arguments of the form: p, if p then q, therefore q.

metaphysics (Greek: after, or beyond, physics, from Aristotle's lecture notes under this heading.) The branch of philosophy that deals with the ultimate constitution of the world. A metaphysical theory does not tell us *why* something is, but *what* it is. A science of the mind (psychology) might offer explanations in neurological terms of human and animal behaviour. But it will not tell us what the mind *is*, or what distinguishes mental from non-mental activity. If the psychologist tells us that mental activity is activity of the brain, then this is not something that his experiments can prove, but a metaphysical adjunct to his science. To prove it, he must give philosophical and not empirical arguments.

moral law The sum of those laws which tell us what is right and what is wrong. Some think that these laws vary from society to society. Others believe that there is a fundamental core of morality that all societies share – perhaps the ten commandments of Mosaic law, or the commandments summarised yet more succinctly in the categorical imperative (q.v.) of Kant.

natural kinds Kinds like the tiger and the oak, or those like water and gold, the instances of which have a common structure or constitution established by their nature; as opposed to artificial kinds like chairs and pictures, which have no common constitution, but merely a common use.

numerical and qualitative identity A is numerically identical with B if A and B are not two things but one. If A and B are two things, but indistinguishable in their qualities, then they are not numerically but qualitatively identical.

obligation An obligation is a duty (q.v.) incurred towards specific people or groups, by virtue of dealings with, or relations to, those people or groups.

optimal See **satisficing**.

perceptual The perceptual aspect of mental life is that concerned with the absorption of information through the senses – e.g. through the eyes (sight) and through the ears (hearing). There is perception only where information can change: hence perception seems to imply learning (q.v.), rather than the merely mechanical response to a stimulus.

philosophy The study of abstract questions concerning the nature of reality, the validity of arguments and the extent of knowledge. Not an empirical (q.v.) science, but an attempt to answer questions which remain when science shuts up. For example: what is science? A good question, but not one that science can answer.

piety (Latin: *pietas*.) The disposition to acknowledge the sacredness and untouchability of things, places, people and customs, not because they are divine, but rather because you have no right to encroach upon them, and because they are intrinsically worthy of respect.

pity The disposition to suffer with other creatures, and to strive to alleviate their pains.

pleasure Two different mental states are described by this term: sensory pleasure, which consists in sensations which we like to have and strive to obtain, and contemplative pleasure, which is a state of mind with intentionality (q.v.). An example of the latter is the pleasure you might take in the sight of your child contentedly playing. Animals feel the first kind of pleasure; do they feel the second? Possibly.

practical reasoning Reasoning about what to do, as opposed to reasoning about what to believe. We reason about the means to achieve our goals. But we also reason about the goals themselves. Morality is an essential premise to this second kind of reasoning.

preference ordering We may not be able to say whether A gives more pleasure than B, but we can empirically determine that Elizabeth prefers A to B under conditions X. We can order preferences in this way: A is preferred under conditions X to B, which is preferred to C etc. This might then give the basis for an econometric system that will enable us to calculate the preferred course of action in a situation where there are potentially conflicting goals. In fact, insuperable paradoxes have been shown to stand in the way of this approach to practical reasoning (q.v.).

pride The attribution of value to oneself, and the disposition to act in such a way that this value is not diminished but enhanced.

proposition The meaning of a sentence and the content (q.v.) of a belief (q.v.).

punishment The infliction of pain in response to, and retribution for, a wrong. In the case of moral beings, punishment is part of the dialogue whereby we bring each other to recognise our wrongs and also to make amends for them. In the case of animals, the wrong in question is not a moral wrong, but an undesirable piece of behaviour, which can be changed by inflicting pain.

reason/reasoning Reason is the capacity to come to theoretical and practical conclusions. It is not the same as reasoning, which is a process, involving step-by-step moves from premise to conclusion. Reason may operate intuitively, as in the moral life, where we spontaneously make judgements without availing ourselves of the reasoning that would justify them, and perhaps without even knowing how that reasoning could be sought for.

remorse The attitude of one who blames himself for something that he has done, believing it to have been morally wrong. Typically the remorseful person seeks to make amends – i.e. to do good to the one he has wronged. Remorse is not the same as guilt, which is private, retreating, and reluctant to confess itself. The guilty person does not seek to make amends, but to hide from the consequences of his action.

resentment Hostility to another person, founded in the belief that he has wronged you or slighted you.

revealed preference A preference displayed by the actual choice of one thing over alternatives, regardless of any countervailing commentary. Thus people have a revealed preference for supermarkets over high-street shops, even though they are loud in condemning the effect of the first in destroying the second.

revenge The wilful damaging of another, in response to damage inflicted on you. Not the same as punishment (q.v.), since not part of the moral dialogue. The person who takes revenge does not want the other to make amends or even to recognise his fault. He wants the other to suffer, preferably more than he has suffered himself. Interestingly, only moral beings seem motivated by revenge, even though revenge in itself need not involve a moral judgement.

right A right is an interest that can be overridden without the consent of the person who possesses it only by doing him a wrong. A right creates a duty to respect it. It is therefore more than a freedom. In claiming a right I am imposing a duty on others; hence the onus is on me to prove that this right exists. In claiming a freedom, I am imposing no duty: the onus is therefore on you to prove that I do not enjoy the freedom that I claim.

satisficing/optimal A solution to a problem is optimal if it is as good as any other; a solution is satisficing if it merely satisfies certain requirements.

scientific inference The inference from the observed phenomena to the hypothesis that explains them.

secular Pertaining to the secular sphere – i.e. the sphere of temporal and mortal things, as opposed to the eternal sphere which is God's. A secular morality is one founded in the facts of human nature, without reference to God.

self-consciousness The ability to identify yourself as 'I', to attribute mental states to yourself, and to engage in dialogue and relations of the I-Thou (q.v.) variety.

self-esteem The attribution to yourself and your life of characteristics that merit respect.

sensory The aspect of mental life that pertains to the senses – i.e. the fundamental organs of awareness, including perceptual (q.v.) organs and the capacity for sensations of pleasure (q.v.) and pain.

sentient An animal is sentient if it has a sensory (q.v.) life. It can be merely sentient, like a mollusc – meaning that it has neither perception (q.v.), nor belief (q.v.), nor desire (q.v.), nor any other of the capacities that make mental life worthwhile.

shame The recognition that your actions are judged adversely by others, and that you too are judged adversely on account of them; together with a disposition to withdraw from the society of those who so judge you. Shame, unlike guilt, may naturally lead to suicide.

sovereignty The absolute right of control over something, which implies that nobody else can meddle with that thing unless with your consent.

theology The study of the divine order of the universe, of the nature of God, and of the conditions laid down on human life by its assumed creator.

utilitarianism The theory that actions are to be assessed in terms of their utility, and that utility should be quantified, for example in terms of pleasure or desire-satisfaction. More generally, any attempt to reduce practical reasoning (q.v.) to some form of cost-benefit analysis (q.v.).

virtue A disposition to choose what is believed to be honourable, right, justified or good, despite the countervailing temptations of appetite, pleasure and desire. Thus courage is the disposition to do what is honourable, despite the promptings of fear; justice the disposition to do what is just, despite the temptations of idleness, self-interest, favouritism and so on; temperance the disposition to do what is right, despite the promptings of sensual desire. And so on.

NOTES

1 Metaphysics

1. Thus, St Thomas Aquinas recognises cruelty to animals as vicious only in so far as it leads to cruelty to human beings. See *Summa Theologica II*, I, Q102, art 6. Aquinas's views have been summarised in Singer, P, *Animal Liberation*, 2nd ed., London, 1990, 193–196; the relevant extracts from Aquinas are contained in Regan, T, and Singer, P, eds, *Animal Rights and Human Obligations*, Englewood Cliffs, 1976. See also the discussion in Barad, J, 'Aquinas' inconsistency on the nature and treatment of animals' in *Between Species*, spring 1988. The official attitude of the medieval church, typified by Aquinas, should be set beside the well-known sympathy for animal life in the writings and teachings of St Francis, whose influence over Christian morality should not be ignored.

2. MacIntyre A, *After Virtue*, London, 1981.

3. Descartes, *Discourse on Method*, Part 5.

4. Ryle, G, *The Concept of Mind*, London, 1949.

5. For a careful examination of ancient writers on this subject, see Sorabji, R, *Animal Minds and Human Morals: the Origins of the Western Debate*, London, 1993. Sorabji offers some telling incidental criticisms of Tom Regan and Peter Singer, and an interesting, if inconclusive, summary of the modern debate.

6. Schopenhauer, A, *The World as Will and Representation*, vol. II, tr. EFJ Payne, New York, 1969, ch. 5.

7. For those interested in a defence of this last claim, I have argued the case at length in *Sexual Desire*, London and New York, 1986.

8. These claims also need more argument than I can give in this place. I have developed the arguments in 'Laughter' and 'Understanding music', both in *The Aesthetic Understanding*, London and Manchester, 1992.

9. See the classic study by von Frisch, K, *Bees: their Vision, Chemical Senses, and Language*, Ithaca, New York, 1951. The idea that the bees have a language has been effectively demolished in Bennett, J, *Rationality*, London, 1964.

2 The moral being

1. See Gauthier, DP, *Morals by Agreement*, Oxford, 1986.

2. See the now famous argument of Ronald Dworkin in 'Taking rights seriously', in his book *Taking Rights Seriously*, London, 1978. It should be said that the concept of a right is hotly disputed in legal and moral philosophy, and my argument is bound to appear contentious. What is not disputed, however, is that only some interests are rights, and that rights are privileged over other interests. This alone is sufficient to undermine the usual case for 'animal rights', which rests purely on the undeniable claim that animals have interests.

3 Life, death, joy and suffering

1. See Singer, P, *Animal Liberation*, London, 1975, 228. Singer himself has grave doubts about this argument, as do other advocates of animal rights. See, for example, Sapontzis, SF, 'On being morally expendable' in *Ethics and Animals*, 1982, vol. 3, 58–72.

2. Clark, SRL, 'How to calculate the greater good' in Paterson, D, and Ryder, RD, eds, *Animals' Rights – a Symposium*, London, 1979.

3. This fact has been much emphasised by Tom Regan, who believes that, rightly understood, it constitutes sufficient ground for according rights to non-human animals. See Regan, T, *The Case for Animal Rights*, Berkeley, California, 1983.

4. Bentham, J, *Introduction to the Principles of Morals and Legislation*, London 1789, ch. XVII, para. 4, fn.

4 The moral margin

1. See the argument in Singer, P, *The Expanding Circle: Ethics and Sociobiology*, Oxford, 1981.

2. This point is enthusiastically argued by Steve Mithen in *The Pre-history of the Mind*, London, 1996.

6 The rational basis of moral judgement
1. Rawls, J, *A Theory of Justice*, Oxford, 1971.

7 The moral status of animals
1. Defenders of bullfighting are adamant that their sport is not sadistic, that it is guided throughout by reverence for the bull, and indeed that the core emotions involved are religious, invoking the kind of sympathy for the tragic hero that is brought before us on the Greek classical stage. On the art, drama and heroism of the bullfight, see Kennedy, AL, *On Bullfighting*, London, 1999.
2. I am conscious that my remarks about zoos do scant justice to the arguments of those who defend them – arguments which have been persuasively summarised in Bostock, S (Education Officer at Glasgow Zoo), *Zoos and Animal Rights*, London, 1994.
3. I should add here that I regard as totally sophistical the argument that fish somehow do not feel pain. This is not because I believe that their nervous system is exactly like ours, but because I believe that pain is not a state of the nervous system. It is to be understood in terms of the connection between injury and pain behaviour, which we observe throughout the animal kingdom. Any argument for saying that fish do not feel pain, simply because their nervous system is differently 'wired', would be an argument for saying that they do not see, do not feel fear, do not feel hunger – in other words, an argument for the Cartesian conclusion that they are a kind of

automaton. Philosophy has entirely exploded such arguments, and they are paraded now only because people have a motive to believe them. In any case, the scientific evidence is very slender, and typified by the findings of Snow, PJ, Plenderleith, MB, and Wright, LL, 'Quantitative study of primary sensory neurone populations of three species of elasmobranch fish' in *Journal of Comparative Neurology*, August 1993, 97–103. The highly speculative results of this study concern the composition of sensory fibres, rather than their functional connections, and therefore assume precisely what needs to be proved. Such arguments, concerning the composition of the nerve fibres in fish, should be set against the accumulated evidence that the functional connection between injury and avoidance is as developed in fish as in mammals, as are the analgesic reactions and effects which we observe in other vertebrates. See Kestin, SC, *Pain and Stress in Fish, a Report to the RSPCA*, amended version, Horsham, 1994. Kestin concludes his persuasive summary with the incontrovertible claim that 'the pain fish feel as a result of injury is likely to be just as important to them in their own way as human pain is to humans'.

4. Although of no philosophical significance, it is important for casuistical purposes to remember that stress inhibits pain – a fact well known from the human battlefield, and confirmed abundantly in the hunting field as well. (See Wall, PM, 'Defining pain in animals' in Short, CE, and Poznak, A, eds, *Animal*

Pain, New York, 1992.) 'Stress-induced analgesia', which is a function of the brain and the spinal cord rather than the local neurones, is vital to all animals which depend on the sensation of pain in order to avert injury. Without it they would lack the ability to save themselves from the most threatening situations, since pain would cripple them. The animal seized in full flight is therefore inherently less likely to feel the extremes of pain suffered by the animal who is clumsily shot while unaware of the danger. Of course, stress which stems from fear is also a form of suffering. But it is the daily lot of animals in the wild, and also a lesser suffering than extreme pain, as is shown by the fact that animals choose the stress of flight against the threat of extreme pain whenever the choice must be made by them.

5. *Guardian*, 21 April 1990.

9 Morality and the law

1. This was written before the introduction of a ban on hand-guns and attempts to ban hunting with hounds. This legislation – driven by majority opinion, without regard for a law-abiding minority – shows the extent to which old-fashioned liberal principles are now being expelled from the political process.

Appendix 2: Thoughts on Hunting

1. Freud, S, *Totem and Taboo,* tr. J Strachey, London, 1950; Malinowski, B, *Sex and Repression in Savage Society*, London, 1963. There is another function

INDEX

abattoirs, closure of local viii,
    143
abortion 136
adultery 136
Aesop 153
aesthetic 175
    and Kant 173
    lack of sense of in animals
        18–19
    meaning 173
affection 32, 33
alienation 173
Anglers' Association 120
angling 112–16, 120, 129, 155
    benefits 171–2
    downside 114
    environmental benefits 112
    and hospitality 159
    moral principles applying to
        112–16
    results if ceased 163
    and returning to natural world
        154
    source of human happiness
        and social institution 111,
        114, 157, 158
    toleration towards 162

    see also fishing
'animal liberation', defenders of
    81
Animal Liberation (Singer) 1
animals
    distinction between people
        and ix, 155–6
    minds of 7–15
    perceived as victim class 2
    principles that should guide us
        in our dealings with 123–6
    raised for meat *see* farm
        animals relating with each
        other 18
antelope 14
anthropomorphism 15, 174
ants 41–2
appetitive 10, 13, 174
Aquinas, St Thomas 16
Aristotle 182
    and happiness 58
    and *psuche* 8
    and rationality 16
    and moral being 132
artificial
    and natural 148, 154
asserted 174

Aufhebung 155, 174–5
aversions 10

badgers x, 109, 140
battery farms 107
Baumgarten, AG 173
bear-baiting 94, 95, 137–8
beasts of burden 88, 89
beautiful 175
beef cattle 100, 104, 144
bees, dance of 25
behavioural continuum 51–2
belief(s) 14, 23
    and animals 10–11, 17–18, 175
    and cognitive 176
    content of 177
    meaning 175
Bentham, Jeremy 48, 57
Blake, William 67
blame
    and utilitarianism 59
'biodiversity' 163
breeding of animals 92
Brophy, Brigid 1
BSE crisis vii–viii, 139–40, 143
Buber, Martin 36, 180
Buffalo Bill 151
bullfighting 94, 96–8, 166
Burke, Edmund 148, 175

calves 103
Cartesian theory of the mind 8,
    25, 175
categorical imperative 29–30, 61,
    69, 175–6, 182
cats viii
cattle farming *see* beef cattle
charity 63, 72, 176
chickens 101, 102
choice 176
citizenship
    extension of shadow
        citizenship to animals
        132–3

Clark, Stephen 43
cod
    disappearance from Atlantic
        167–8
cognitive 10–12, 176
common law 71, 176–7
communication 25 *see also*
    language
communities 28–30
conditioning 11, 177
consciousness 20–1, 177 *see also*
    self-consciousness
contnet 177
cost-benefit analysis 177, 178
culling 62, 111, 163
culture
    and nature 147
Czech *samizdat* cartoon 103

Darwinian theory 7
death 45, 46–7
decision theory 178
deer 109
    culling of 162
    idea of introducing wolves as
        means of controlling
        113–14
deer-hunting ix, 113–14
Demos vii, 201
Descartes, René 175
    and Caretesian theory of the
        mind 175
    sees animals as merely
        automata 8, 20
desire(s) 10, 13–14, 17, 176, 177,
    178
dietary laws 139
dilemma 77
dog-fighting 94, 95, 137–8
dogs 41, 136
    breeding of 92
    life-long attachment formed
        with humans 83
    social feelings 15

dolphins 22–3, 26
domestic animals *see* pets
duty (duties)
 conflicting of 77
 meaning 178
 and morality 30–2, 62, 70, 156
 obligation as a 183
 to animals 82, 124, 125

Eastern Europe 159
elephants 22–3
emotion(s)
 and animals 14–15
 and language 24
 meaning 178
 and moral beings 34–5
empirical 178
Enlightenment 4, 27, 66, 175,
  178–9
environment
 benefits of angling 112
 duty of care towards 130
 sentimentality as unfavourable
  to 130–1
environmental movements 150
equality, moral 70
erotic love 14, 179
ethology 179
Exmoor 162
experiments on animals 106–8,
  125–6
exploitation
 types of animals used by
  humans 88

farm animals 125–6, 139–45
 and BSE crisis vii–viii,
  139–40, 143
 conditions in which they are
  raised 100, 101–3, 126, 141
 and eating of meat 96, 99–105
 manner of death 142–3
 relationship with man vii, 144
 and timing of killing 103–4,
  142–3
farmers 105
 and the hunt 145, 159–60
 and ramblers 159–60
 relationship with animals vii,
  144
favouritism 63
 extended to certain animal
  species 5–6, 109–10
fear 178
 infliction of 95
'field sports' 157–8
fish
 and feeling of pain 194 5n
 lack of sympathy towards 4,
  111, 165
fish-factories 171
fish-farming 170
fishing 165–72
 depletion of stocks 167–9
 disappearance of cod from
  Atlantic 167–8
 industrial fishing as offence to
  totem 154–5
 solution to disappearance of
  stocks 169, 170, 171–2
 see also angling
fox-hunting ix, 116-22, 164
 contribution to balance of
  nature and landscape
  116–17
 and the farmer 145, 159–60
 objections to 116, 119
 role in rural community 120–1
 source of social life and
  happiness 117
 see also hunting
foxes x, 129, 162
French Revolutionaries 158–9
From the House of the Dead
  (Janáček) 166
fur farms
 releasing of mink from viii,
  130

game laws 158
Geist 149, 179
Genesis 149
genetic engineering 92
glossary 173–89
goldfish 166
grass-snakea x
gratitude 179–80
guilt 186

happiness
   meaning 180
   and utilitarianism 58
Hattersley, Roy 119, 120
Hegel, Georg Wilhelm Friedrich
   16, 52
   and *Geist* 149, 179
   Phenomenology of Spirit 24
Heimkehr 150, 161
Hindu tradition 99, 100
Hitler, Adolf 59, 86
Hölderlin, Johann 149
Holy Will 180
horse-racing 89–90, 90–1, 93,
   114
horses 25, 83, 88, 89
   conception of individuality of
      other members 39
   and desire 13–14
   mare-foal attachment 36
   and social feelings–15
hospitality and hunting 159–60
humility 65
humour animals and lack of 19
hunter-gatherer 151–2, 153,
   156–7, 158
hunting vii, 111, 125, 129–30,
   147–64
   arguments against 161–2
   dependence on ethic of combat
      115
   and farmers 145, 159–60
   and hospitality 159–60
   and returning to natural world

154, 161
   revival of long-buried
      emotions of our forebears
      161
   social artefact 157–8
   as territorial activity 158–9
   and totemism 151–2, 154, 155,
      157, 197n
   treatment of animals as
      individuals 153
   see also fox-hunting
Huxley, Aldous 91

I-Thou (*Ich-Du*) 36, 180, 187
Icelanders 168, 169
imagination 18, 180
imbeciles 54, 55
indignation 19, 181
individuality 39–44
infanticide 54
infants 53, 55
injustice 181
insects
   and aversion 14
   lack of sympathy towards 4,
      111, 125
   and perception 13
intentionality 12, 124, 176, 181,
   184
International Fund for Animal
   Welfare ix

Janáček, Leos
   From the House of the Dead
      166
Jefferies, Richard 154
Jewish law 139
Jorrocks 121
Judaeo-Hellenic tradition 99
justice 59, 63, 156, 181

kangaroo 109
Kant, Immanuel 43, 61
   and aesthetic 173

and categorical imperative 29–30, 69, 175–6, 182
and concept of the person 27
on maternal attachment in animals 35
moral philosophy 21, 30, 180
and rationality 16
and sublime 148
Kantians 64
kindness 63
Kurlansky, Mark 167

La Fontaine, Jean de 153
land ownership 159
language 19, 23–6
law and morality 133, 135–8
Laws, *The* (Plato) 118, 164
learning 11, 177, 181
livestock *see* farm animals
lizards 6
logical connectives 181

MacIntyre, Alasdair 4
mad cow disease *see* BSE crisis
MAFF viii, 143
marginal humans 52–6, 68
Masters of Fox-Hounds Association 120
maternal attachment 35–6
meat, eating of *see* farm animals
medical research and live experimentation 106–8
Melville, Herman 166
mercy killing 78
Metamorphoses (Ovid) 152
metaphysics 1–26, 182
Mill, John Stuart 57
mind, Cartesian theory of 8, 25, 175
mink x
  results of release into wild viii, 130–1
mink-hounds 131

Moby Dick (Melville) 166
moral equality 70
moral law 38, 43, 60–1, 63, 69–71, 76–7
  and Kant's categorical imperative 29–30, 61, 69, 175–6, 182
  meaning 182
  need for absolute component 62
  persons and 30–2
  principles of 69–70
  and utilitarianism 74
  virtue as source of 54, 62–4, 69, 71, 73 4, 84, 124
moral life 32–8
morality (moral thinking) 2–3, 4, 49, 57–68, 77–8
  and citizenship 132–3
  essential function of 77
  and the law 133, 135–8
  motive of 76
  and piety *see* piety
  responding to conflicts 76–8
  and sympathy *see* sympathy
  and utilitarianism 57–60
Muslims
  and ritual slaughter 96
mutton 104
myths 151

natural
  and artificial 148, 154
natural kinds 182
'natural law' 70
natural order
  desire for 149
  humans as guardians of 162
nature 147–8
  and culture 147
  and Rousseau 149
  unity with 150–1
  unkindness to animals 47
negotiation(s) 28, 29

shaping of moral community
32
Nietzsche, Friedrich Wilheim
36, 37
non-moral beings 79–83, 123–4
need to distinguish between
moral
and 123–4
numerical identity 183

obligation 183
Ovid
Metamorphoses 152

pain
feeling of by fish 194–5n
feelings of 48–9
inflicting of 94–8
and punishment 49
and stress 195–6n
Paradise 149
Pavlov, Ivan Petrovich 177
People for the Ethical Treatment
of Animals (PETA) ix
perception
animals and 9–10, 13
meaning 183
person, concept of 27–30, 28, 80
personality 27–30, 69
pest-control 163
pests
division between pets and x
PETA (People for the Ethical
Treatment of Animals) ix
pets 44, 82, 83–8, 153
dependence on humans 87
division between pests and x
enhancement of virtues and
vices of their owners 86
needs 85
responsibilities and duties
towards 83–4
Phenomenology of Spirit (Hegel)
24

philosophy 183
piety 54, 64–8, 69, 78, 92, 124
and dietary laws 139
and eating of meat 99
meaning 65, 183–4
need to respect feelings of 67
and reason 65, 75
and 'reflective equilibrium'
75–6
pigs 101
Pillow Book, The (Shonagon) 81
pity 36–7, 184
Plato 16
The Laws 118, 164
pleasure 36, 184
polo 89–90
pornography 137, 138
practical reasoning 184, 185
preference, revealed 186
preference ordering 184–5
pride 185
primates 7
proposition 185
psuche 8
punishment 185, 186
administered during training
17
necessity of 49

qualitative identity 183

ramblers
farmers' attitude to 159–60
Ramblers' Association 159
rationality 16–20, 51, 53, 60–1
rats x, 129
human revulsion for 5–6, 109
reason 16, 22, 66, 185
and piety 65, 75
reasoning 185
'reflective equilibrium' 75–6
Regan, Tom 2, 52, 53
religious belief
decline in as factor for

prominence of animal
    welfare 3
remembering 18
remorse 186
reptiles, reaction to 4
resentment 186
responsibility
    and utilitarianism 59–60
revealed preference 186
revenge 186
right(s) 30–1, 31–2, 156, 181
    and animals 1–2, 124
    conflict of 77
    meaning 187
    and moral law 30–1, 31–2, 61,
        62, 70
    problems with ascribing to
        animals 80–1
Rilke, Rainer Maria 83
ritual slaughter 96, 135
Roman law 27
Romans 64
Rousseau, Jean Jacques 149
RSPCA (Royal Society for the
    Prevention of Cruelty to
    Animals) ix, 133
Ryder, Richard 1, 2
Ryle, Gilbert 8

satisficing 187
Schelling, Friedrich 149
Schopenhauer, Arthur 18
scientific inference 187
seal-hunting ix
secularisation 4, 187
self-consciousness 20–3, 24–5,
        35, 36, 51, 53, 155–6, 177
    and animals 22–3, 44, 177
    distinguishing from
        consciousness 21
    meaning 187
self-esteem 187
sensations
    feeling of by animals 9

sensory 9, 188
sentient 188
sentimentality 126–31, 140
    confusion with real love 127
    unfavourable to ecology and
        environment 130–1
    as a vice 127–8
sexual stimulus 10, 14
shame 188
sharks 166
sheep 83, 100, 104
Shonagon, Sei
    The Pillow Book 81
shooting 125, 157, 159
signs
    communication through 25
Singer, Peter 2, 52, 81, 123
    Animal Liberation 1, 90
    distinction between animals
        which do and do not exist
        as individuals 40
skate
    extinction of in North Sea
        168–9
slaughtering 142–3
    closure of small abattoirs vii,
        143
    ritual 96, 135
    of young animals 104
snakes 6
social feelings
    and animals 15
sovereignty 156, 188
Spanish fishermen 168
'speciesism' 1–2
species-soul, idea of 152
speech see language
spiders x
sporting events
    animals used in 88, 89–90,
        92–3
squirrels 17
Stravinsky, Igor 153
stress

and pain 195–6n
sublime 148, 175
suffering 48–50, 81
Surtees, RS 121, 153
swordfish 166
symbolic behaviour 26
sympathy 33, 36, 37, 61–2, 62–3,
    69, 72–5, 124, 128
  competing with piety 78
  and detachment from moral
    order 35
  and utilitarianism 72, 73,
    74–5, 77–8, 124

theology 179, 188
toads 6
totemism 151–2, 154, 155, 157,
    197n
training of animals 17, 95
trapping 131

utilitarianism 48, 49, 57–60, 64,
    65, 82, 87, 95
  attraction of 76
  and cost-benefit analysis 177,
    189
  inability to explain distinction
    between animals and
    people 57–8
  meaning 188–9
  morality and moral law
    57–60, 74
  objections to 58–60
  and sympathy 72, 73, 74–5,
    77–8, 124

true motive of thinking 74

Vale of White Horse 160
virtue(s) 90, 181
  characteristics 33–4, 63
  feelings associated with 36
  meaning 189
  as source of moral law 54,
    62–4, 69, 71, 73–4, 84, 124

Walton, Isaak 154
Washoe (chimpanzee) 25, 26
waterways 130–1
whales 166
wild animals 108–22, 148
  destruction of habitats ix
  duties and responsibilities
    towards 82, 108–9, 125
  favouritism extended to
    certain species 109–10
  looked on unsympathetically
    128
  nature's unkindness to 47
  principles for moral attitude
    towards 111–12
  species lying beyond reach of
    natural sympathy 110–11
Wittgenstein, Ludwig 25
  Philosophical Investigations 24
wolves
  idea of introducing as means
    of controlling deer 113–14

zoos 88, 98–9, 125